ALL BUT MY LIFE

"I took a very great deal out of motor-racing, but I put a lot back, too. I do feel that I gave it all but my life."

I HOPE that this book conveys, as we have tried to make it do, some of the complexities of the world of motor-racing, and one man's life in that world. The book has not been in the ordinary sense a project, a labour. There has been little about it that was arduous. It has been an enjoyment. It is unusual that two people, finishing a work of this kind, with its numerous opportunities for disagreement and argument, find themselves closer in friendship than they were when they began it, but that is the present case.

Ken W. Purdy

I T would be hard for me to exaggerate, in saying how much I owe to motor racing. It has been an exciting and rewarding profession. It has taken me around the world and through it I have met many people who have deeply influenced me, and whom I have enjoyed knowing.

Obviously it is a great disappointment to me to have to give up the Sport, but I know that to continue would be too frustrating to bear. I believe that I am still reasonably competent but I know that in Grand Prix racing I would not be satisfied with the performances I would most likely give. Competition has been a great source of exhilaration to me but I am a perfectionist, and I am sure I would not be satisfied starting in a race knowing that I would not be able to equal those performances I formerly considered my standard.

I certainly have no ground for complaint when I think back upon what motor-racing has been in my life. I hope that in the future, tomorrow, if you like, or the day afterwards, I shall be able to make a return to the Sport in some way, to try to give back something of what it has given me.

CONTENTS

ILLUSTRATIONS

CHAPTER I

"There is a splendour to racing which no other
work can match. . . ."

Robert Daley

CHAPTER I

A PRETTY nurse pushed him into the room, riding a high-backed, old-fashioned wheel-chair, a small man, heavily-muscled, laughing, slit-eyed. This was his forty-sixth day in the hospital, and for most of those days he had been unconscious, or semi-conscious, or in amnesia, but he was tanned and he looked strong. The left side of his face was raddled with rough, red scars around the eye, as if someone had gone after him with a broken beer-bottle.

"That was a funny story, boy, in your last letter," he said, "that story about the clam-digger . . . what's this, what's this?" An enchanting *gamine* thing in faded levis red-brown hair and dark glasses was handing him an envelope, her photograph. "I *like* that!" he said. "Put it over there; stand it up. This is Judy Carne . . . you've met, you two?"

We had met. He stared at her, smiling. His eyes were not working in parallel, he appeared to have to point his head directly at whatever he wanted to see. He grabbed her wrist.

"Did *you* see the *Daily Sketch* yesterday?" He turned to me. "Did you see that, boy? We were sitting in the garden, this bloke poked a telephoto lens over the wall, the bastard was twenty yards away, Judy was brushing a bread-crumb off my chin when he shot it, 'an admirer' the caption said. . . ."

"I like *that*," Miss Carne said. " 'Admirer!' "

"Are you suing?"

"I can't," she said. "I'm going to Hollywood tomorrow."

He smiled again. He looked much as he had when I saw him four days before he went off the course at around 120 miles an hour and slammed into a bank at the Goodwood race circuit; the forty-odd stitches had been taken out of his face; the left cheek-bone, stuffed full of support from inside, didn't betray that it had been shattered, and his nose didn't really look as if it had ever been broken, much less broken eight times. His bare left foot lay immobile on the wheel-chair rest. His leg was bandaged, but the plaster cast was on the window-sill, sliced in two. There were marks on the pink top of his head. He looked beat-up but whole. What he could move, he did move: his head, his right arm, his left arm, less, and he talked. He picked up a cellophane bag of red roses someone had left on the bed.

"They're from Germany," he said. He read the name. "I don't know who that is," he said. He heard the door open behind him. "Viper?" he said. He looked around the back of the wheel-chair. "Viper, you went off with my fountain-pen."

Valerie Pirie, his secretary, a calm, pretty girl, bright-eyed, quick, intelligent. She gave him his pen. He made a note on the card and dropped it on a neat pile of cards and letters.

"So-and-so and so-and-so are outside," Valerie said. "I told them not to come, but . . . and the man from Grundig is coming at four-thirty, about the tape-recorder."

An orderly brought in another bunch of red roses. As he left, a tall blonde came in; behind her, another, taller. Kiss-kiss. Judy Carne was lying on the bed, her chin in her hand.

"I'll tell you, boy," he was saying to me, "nothing that has happened since I came here, except when they broke my nose again, to re-set it, hurt like that clot's shaving me. I had seven days' growth of beard. He swore he knew how. I can't think where he'd learned, it was like pulling it out. I asked him if he had another razor, he said, yes, why, and I told him I thought he should give me a chance to defend myself. . . ."

Another nurse, with tea, bread and butter, jam, clotted cream. He talked. Valerie said: "Drink your tea, Stirling." He made a face at her, but he drank it, and she gave him another cup. He made each of the blondes eat a piece of bread and butter and jam. Neither wanted to, they were dieting, but they couldn't think of answers for the persuasions that poured out of him. When they had conceded, he went to another subject without a perceptible pause.

He said to me: "You know, I'm not supposed to put any weight on this left leg, under penalty of death or flogging or something, but I'll tell you, the other night I went from there, to there, the wash-basin, *and* back, actually coming back I passed out, I didn't go unconscious, I get dizzy now and then, I just fell down, but it was so funny—the reason I had to do it, you see, I had been trapped by a damned stupid designer, actually, the clot, whoever the devil he was, who designed the standard male urinal, you know you *cannot* set the thing down if it's full beyond a certain level, it's ridiculous, when I get out of here I shall design a new one, I'll wager this one hasn't been changed since 1890...."

He talked very well, but he didn't stop. For some time after the accident, his words, when he spoke in delirium, were thick and slurred because of the brain injury, and there was some reason to doubt he would ever speak clearly again. Worse, Rob Walker, his patron and his friend, whose car he had been driving when he crashed, had said: "I have the impression that he cannot form an idea of his own, but can only respond to ideas that are fed to him." In talking about one of Moss's own cars, for example, Walker had discovered that Stirling did not know that he owned it, although it had been his for some time; he said that he had at one time considered buying such a car, but had abandoned the idea.

Now he spoke the crisp quick English he had always used, and ideas seemed to come as fast as he could handle them. And he went on and on. It wasn't that he talked incessantly, or compulsively, although he did come close. He would stop to listen. But he would be silent only exactly as long as someone spoke, and had something to speak about. Then he would begin instantly to talk again. There were no pauses. I think he was happy to find himself *able* to talk again, and in any case excitation is common in recovery from severe trauma. But it was plain that he wanted no silences in that room.

I remembered something he had said the last time I'd seen him before the accident, four days before it, in a long dark afternoon of talk in the little flat in Earl's Court Road: "When I go to bed tonight, I hope to be tired, very tired, because I don't want to think. I don't want to think."

Valerie Pirie had said to me, when he was still in coma —she was one of the people who took turns sitting beside his bed twenty-four hours a day—"Do you know, last night he was speaking in French and Italian, as well as English, of course, but his accent in French and Italian was very pure, much better than it's ever been when he was conscious. Why's that, do you think?"

"Disinhibition, I'm sure. What did he say?"

"He was talking about girls a lot of the time. Once he said: '*E molto difficile per un corridore—molto difficile.*'" ("[Life] is very hard for a race-driver—very hard.")

Stirling Moss's life a hard life? Not many would have

thought so. Stirling Moss is one of the best-known men in the world, and beyond any doubt the best-known sports figure. Sonny Liston, the heavyweight boxing champion, is famous in the United States; Tex Dexter, the cricketer, is a familiar figure in the United Kingdom and Australia and New Zealand—but there are tens of thousand of Swedes and Portuguese and Argentinians and Canadians who have watched Stirling Moss drive, and not once, but many times. He is instantly recognized in Rome or Nairobi or Tokyo. For years his income has run around £50,000 a year. He knows the world as few men know it. He travels constantly, once flew from South Africa to Australia to see a girl, flew back next day. Injuries aside, he is healthy as a bull, iron-hard, capable of fantastic endurance. Some of his friends claim that they have never seen him tired. He likes sports and is competent in most that he has tried and superior in some. For example, his sister, Pat, said that Stirling was a better show-rider and jumper at sixteen than she is today, and she was one of the world's leading riders, a member of the British International team, when she made the remark. (As teen-age performers, the two of them once cleaned out an entire horse-show; between them they won every prize offered. Their father, embarrassed, put up a cup and excluded them from competing for it.) Moss is intelligent, easily aroused to intense interest in almost anything. Although he says that he considers his fund of general information to be low, and his ability to retain new knowledge not very high, he will learn about anything that he thinks will be useful, a typical assortment being sound-proofing, commercial laundry operation, neurology. He is a sought-after television and radio guest. He is an amusing and fluent speaker, a skill he forced himself to learn, and a painful and laborious business it was, because by nature he is introverted and very shy. But he is good at it now, and I have seen him hold the absorbed attention of a thousand people in a New York banquet-hall. In some years he has made a hundred such appearances. He has, for example, presided over the opening of four new petrol-stations in one day, flying from city to city in a British Petroleum helicopter. Five successful books on racing and some eight hundred magazine and newspaper articles have appeared under his by-line. He subscribes to no clipping service, but he has forty-seven full scrapbooks, nevertheless. His mail runs to 10,000 pieces a year and he answers every letter, and promptly. Most men like him. Women find him attractive, nine times in ten. He is rarely without a woman companion, often has two or three dates in a single day—and this although he has little confidence in himself, and sometimes finds it hard to bring himself to ask a girl to dance. His shyness is real, it is painful, there is nothing simulated about it, but it seems little warranted: women who have known him testify extravagantly on his presence, kindness, thoughtfulness, gentleness, concentration, and the ultimate mark is on him: his women know that he has other women and they don't care. After all, if he hasn't seen a woman for a year, and she has changed her coiffure, he is likely to remark on it. To many women, diamonds are less than this.

Most importantly, he has, all his life, had work to do which he has liked doing, and in the common judgment of his peers he is better in his work than any other man alive. Asked if he considered himself the best racing-driver in the world, the present champion, Graham Hill, said that he did not. "Stirling Moss is," Hill said, "or was." He may be the greatest race-driver of all time, the greatest who has lived. I make this statement reluctantly, and with great care, and not upon my own recognizance. I am not expert

in this field. I am no eminent authority. I have seen Stirling
Moss drive, and I have seen the only other drivers who are
ever seriously mentioned in the same breath with him, Tazio
Nuvolari, who died in 1953; Rudolf Caracciola, who died
in 1959; and Juan Manuel Fangio, who retired in 1958. I
have seen Alberto Ascari and Bernd Rosemeyer and Richard
Seaman and very many others. I think perhaps I have seen,
since 1935, everyone who was of the first rank in the most
dangerous and demanding sport man has been able to devise
for himself, motor-racing, and, of them, I think Stirling
Moss is best. But little weight need be attached to my
opinion, because I have not followed the sport year after
year, race after race, missing nothing. There are those who
have: Enzo Ferrari, racing-driver, team-manager, manufacturer of the car that has won more races than anything
else man has ever set upon wheels, certainly the most eminent authority on racing active today, was asked, in
December 1962, eight months after Moss's last race, whom
he thought the greatest driver in the world. He replied
quickly. "Stirling Moss," he said. "And he is the only one
who can be compared with Nuvolari."

Juan Manuel Fangio, five times champion of the world,
drove many races against Moss. He is an intelligent, sensitive, kindly man, and there are many who think that he
was incomparable as a driver. Fangio says: "Moss was the
best, in my time."

Moss has entered more races than anyone else ever did,
and won more. He has won so many silver cups that he
estimates they could be melted down into an ingot that
would weigh three hundred pounds. (The ingot, he thinks,
would in turn make a striking coffee table.) There is no
accounting of his store of other awards, medals, trophies, including such rarities as the golden *Coupe des Alpes,* given

for three consecutive victories in the Alpine Rally; men have spent fifteen years trying to win *one* Alpine. I remember seeing Moss at Bobby Said's house in Pound Ridge, New York, when he was on his way home after a race in Venezuela, carrying the Perez Jiminez Cup, a lump of solid gold so heavy it was unpleasant to hold in one hand.

For years he has been conceded the fastest and most versatile driver alive and that he has never won the championship of the world is one of the major curiosities of sport—and perhaps a minor curiosity of psychology, too. When he told me what he would do if, today, he found himself winning the world championship, I felt my hair rise —but that must come later. He has been three times third in the world rankings, four times second. The championship is decided on the basis of placement in eight to ten major races throughout the world. In one year Moss won four of these races but lost the championship to a man who won only one but who was placed in more races than Moss. Moss's insistence on driving, when possible, privately-owned cars (factory-owned models are always faster) of British manufacture has severely handicapped him. (As this was written, British cars were the fastest in the world; in the 1950's they emphatically were not.) But Moss has beaten every man who has held the world championship for the past ten years. He is one of the few, the very few, of whom it can truly be said that they do the one thing, whatever it is, better than anyone else can do it. These men are forever set apart. In his profession Moss is an immortal. And he is thirty-three, well off if not rich, healthy, popular, talented to an extreme, a citizen of the world.

E molto difficile per un corridore—molto difficile?

Yes. Very difficult. And the higher one is placed, the more difficult. The essence of the difficulty is that motor-racing on the highest level, in the fastest, most competitive company, *grand prix* driving, is the most dangerous sport in the world. It is one of the riskiest of man's activities. Motor-racing kills men. In one recent year the mortality rate was twenty-five per cent, or one out of four. These are odds to be compared with those cited for fighter pilots and paratroopers. The list of competition drivers killed since 1946 was, as this was written, approximately 175. Of these, perhaps fifty were major figures.

If the game is so dangerous, why does anyone play it?

Because it's the most compelling, delightful, sensuously rewarding game in the world. A strong statement? Yes. But if motor-racing is not the most exciting competitive game a man can play, what is? The stick-and-ball games? Exercises, pastimes, demanding, yes, if you like, but still, games that children can play. A century in Test cricket, a 30-foot putt dropped for a birdie at St. Andrews or Pebble Beach, a home run with the bases loaded in a World Series—these are great accomplishments, pinnacles of excitement to players and spectators—but they can be only trifling, if interesting, incidents to men who have driven 160-mile-an-hour automobiles through the hills and the unnumbered corners of the Nurburg Ring, fourteen miles to the lap, flat-out in rain and fog. The world does not produce, in a year, more than a handful of men, fifteen or twenty at the most, skilful enough, and competitive enough, to play this game, and of this handful, only a third, perhaps even fewer, will be of the very first rank.

Some stick-and-ball games, like real tennis, or *jeu de paume,* are both physically and intellectually demanding, as motor-racing is, but a split-second miscalculation in real tennis will cost only a point, not a life, or crippling, or sixty days in hospital. Bull-fighters, mountain-climbers, skindivers know something of the race-driver's ecstasy, but only a part, because theirs are team-sports. *Toreros* are never alone and mountaineers rarely; the skin-diver not usually, and in any case his opponent, the sea, though implacable and deadly, still is passive. When a racing-car is passive it is sitting in the garage, and its driver's seat is as safe as a baby's cradle.

What is a racing-driver? Is any man who has learned to drive at 150 miles an hour reasonably well through traffic, a racing-driver? No, he isn't. Hear Moss: "If you habitually go through the corners one-fifth of a second slower than your maximum, you can make a reputation, you can earn a living, you can even win a race now and then—but you are no racing-driver."

There are many such, and there are many drivers who deny that there is anything aesthetically or sensuously rewarding about motor-racing. But they betray themselves when they say, and they all do: "I drive because I like it" or "I like the life". They feel, yes, but they are inarticulate. Understandably, these drivers are annoyed when extreme sensitivity is attributed to men who are, after all, doing the same thing they're doing. These drivers sometimes write chiding, but always courteous notes of complaint to writers who have annoyed them in this way. "You are making the thing over-dramatic," they'll say. "It's not that important. A chauffeur is just a chauffeur, after all, some go faster than others."

On the other side of the coin, drivers of Moss's stripe sometimes get angry with writers who do not understand the *métier*. I have known Moss to be harsh and brusque to a journalist he thought stupid. Phil Hill is another who will not suffer fools gladly. No one more intelligent than Phil Hill ever held the wheel of a racing-car, and probably no one more sensitive to the world around him, either. Seeing

Hill, just after a four-hour driving stint in darkness and pouring rain at Sebring, almost visibly recoil at the profound asinity of the question: "What's it feel like out there?" is to see the depths of frustration clear and plain. Still, all he said was: "My God, what kind of question is *that*?"

No, racing-drivers are not all the same, any more than other men sharing the same pursuit. Yehudi Menuhin and the first violinist of a provincial Polish symphony orchestra play the same instrument, but there the similarity ends.

The full terror and the full reward of this fantastic game, motor-racing, are given only to those who bring to the car talent honed by obsessive practice into great skill, a fiercely competitive will and high intelligence, with the flagellating sensitivity that so often accompanies it. In these men, a terrible and profound change sometimes takes place: the game becomes life. They understand what Karl Wallenda meant when he said, going back up to the high wire after the tragic fall in Detroit that killed two of his troupe and left another a paraplegic: "To be on the wire is life; the rest is waiting."

This change is irreversible. A man who has gone through it will never come back across the fence to the herd. Once the game has become life, and life has become a vestibule, great courage is required to renounce the game—because renunciation is almost suicide. Tazio Nuvolari, for decades called the greatest master of racing-driving, could not find the courage to leave the game that had broken almost every major bone in his body and had time after time brought doctors formally to announce that his death impended; he drove with blood running down his chin because the exhaust-fumes had so irritated his lungs as to cause haemorrhage; he drove when he was so weak he had to be lifted, helpless, from the car at the end of a race; he drove until he could not drive; he died in bed, hating it.

No, *grand prix* racing has nothing to do with other games, just as driving a *grand prix* car has nothing to do with driving a Jaguar or a Chrysler on a motorway, even at a hundred miles an hour. ("It has not to *do* with it," Moss says. "That kind of driving is not even remotely the same thing. It's night and day, fire and water.")

Juan Manuel Fangio retired because he was slowing and because he was depressed by the thought of the drivers he had known who had been killed. No one who remembers the profound grief in Fangio's face, his arms around the sobbing Froilan Gonzalez the day their friend and compatriot Onefre Marimon was killed in 1954, can question the pain motor-racing brought to him, though it made him a world-figure and a millionaire. But, for all that it is so far behind him now, I think that today, if he were standing in front of the pits on a practice day and someone were to point to a car and say: "Juan Manuel, that is your car, made for you, to your measurements, set up for you"—I think the struggle within the man would be a hard one.

Men like Nuvolari and Fangio—or the *matador de toros* Juan Belmonte, retiring with the ridged scars of uncounted bull-gorings on a thin, frail body—share a common mould: skill, obsession, courage, sensitivity. Courage doesn't count most. Skill is basic, more than skill, rather that which one can have only through the accident of heredity, talent; talent, and sensitivity, and always the obsession. When the obsession is great enough, the man will find courage to sustain it, somewhere. The American race-driver Frank Lockhart, killed at Daytona in 1928, often vomited before he got into the car, but he got into it.

For these men, the play's the thing. The game counts.

Driving is for driving's sake, and for winning, even when losing. We may never know the technical reason for Stirling Moss's crash at Goodwood, whether the car failed or he failed, but the basic reason is clear enough; it was Moss's bone-deep conviction that professional driving is *fast* driving, fast, flat-out, nine-tenths of maximum even running dead last without a chance in a hundred of winning. Since 1893, probably no driver, with the single exception of Wilbur Shaw, three times a winner at Indianapolis, has made as much money out of racing as Moss has, but money-making has never been his basic purpose, nor was it Shaw's. Nothing so simple.

No one has a right to disparage *any* driver, I think. If a man has enough courage to get into the car, with the intention of *trying* to get up in front, he has set himself apart. (Stirling disagrees with me on this. "I am *not* braver than the next chap," he said. "I never felt that it took courage to get into the car.") But many have raced, and are racing today, who think of the things the sport can bring besides the satisfaction of doing it. This is their right. Why shouldn't a man plan to achieve fame in one endeavour so as to use it in another? Some may plan business careers, some may have other ideas. The Marquis de Portago, that gay and moody man who amused himself in so many ways, not least by building up a reputation as rake-hell and Casanova, intended to use racing as a springboard to a political career in Spain. When I asked him if he would go on racing, should he win the world championship, he laughed. "Not for a minute!" he said.

Portago wanted to be Foreign Minister of Spain, and, considering that King Alfonso XIII was his godfather and that his forebears had served Spanish governments since the 14th century, it was no doubt an ambition within his realization.

27

As for the other man, the one for whom driving is its own justification, the man who has gone over, the man for whom Karl Wallenda was speaking, the one for whom the game is life, the terror of his nights will be, not mortal death, which he will have seen many times, and which, like a soldier, he believes is most likely to take the man next to him, and the risk of which is in any case the price of admission to the game, not mortal death, but real death— final deprivation of the right to go up on the wire again. Then, like Moss, he'll do anything to get back. In the hospital Moss would accept any pain, any kind of treatment, anything at all that he could believe would shorten, if only by a little, his path back to the racing-car, never mind the fact that a crew of mechanics sweated forty minutes with hacksaws and metal-shears to cut the last one apart enough to make it let go of him. When he was finally lifted free his face was slashed to the bone, his left cheekbone crushed, his eye-socket displaced, his left arm broken, his leg broken at knee and ankle and badly cut, his nose broken, muscles torn, and his brain so massively bruised that the left side of his body was paralysed.

"Recovery from the brain damage is likely to be a slow process," specialists said, "and there is a possibility that full recovery of function in the arm and leg will not take place."

When he had come back to consciousness and had been told what day it was, and what month, and the condition he was in, Moss began, in the night, and whenever he could, to move the broken leg to exercise it. For a long time he couldn't tell if it was moving or not, but he tried.

"I'm afraid of death," he has said to me more than once. "I'm afraid to die, but I'm not afraid of pain. In the hospital this time, and the other time, after Spa, I've exercised what I could, and pushed as hard as I could, until I was just this side of exhaustion, just this side of passing out. That's the only way to do it, boy. No exercise is any good if you don't take it right to the absolute limit. It was applied intelligence that brought Roger Bannister to the four-minute mile, knowing the length of his stride to a millimetre, the weight of his shoes to a fraction of an ounce—but also it was his ability to pace himself so that he crossed the finish line totally exhausted, every bit of energy used up in the running, not enough left to keep him on his feet, barely enough left to keep him alive. That's how it has to be."

How does a man come to this terrible place?

By an ordinary road, usually.

Moss's father, Alfred Moss, is a prosperous London dentist. He was a race-driver, although never approaching the first rank. Still, he ran at Indianapolis in 1924, and he did some barn-storming in the United States, sliding the dusty dirt-tracks in the county fair circuit. ("Maybe that's why he over-steers when he's driving," Stirling says. "I always try to see to it my father has an understeering car. He makes me nervous when I'm driving with him, he always oversteers just a bit.")*

It's a cliché in psychology that the son of a famous father will probably have a troubled life—and so will the son of a man who didn't quite make the top in dangerous or competitive pursuit. In the first instance, the son tries to equal, and if possible exceed his father's accomplishments. In the second instance, the father tries to drive his son, at whatever cost, to do what he could not do. In each case, tragedy is likely. Anyone in car-racing today can name at least one current example of each phenomenon. It has seemed re-

---

*An understeering car has an inherent design tendency to go straight in a corner, instead of following the front wheels around; an oversteering car has an inherent tendency to go more sharply into the corner, to bring the rear end around. A skilled driver can produce either characteristic at will.

markable to me that Stirling Moss's father did not appear, at the beginning, to want his son to go into racing, and that he has not taken more than normal paternal pride in Stirling's triumphs. He has never seemed to relate his career at the wheel to his son's, except as a matter of curiosity and coincidence. He has shown unusual balance.

Stirling's mother, Aileen Moss, was a driver, too. Mrs. Moss was a well-known competitor in rallies, and in 1936 she was woman champion of England. She drove a Marendaz, one of the specialist cars for which England was famous, a high-performance motor-car built from 1926 to 1936. She was a noted horsewoman, too. Stirling was the first of the two Moss children, born September 17, 1929.

Stirling was no great success as a student. He was bright, but indifferent to the academic appeal. He was the kind of problem student who requires teaching of special skill and sympathy, and apparently he didn't get it. He was often ill. His medical record shows appendicitis as a child, and a serious, prolonged case of nephritis, which was later to keep him out of the Royal Air Force. He and the academic life abandoned each other when he was in his late teens; he tried apprenticing himself to hotel administration and to farming—the Moss family home, in Tring, Hertfordshire, is run as a farm—but he was bored.

He could drive an automobile, in the sense of steering it, when he was six. He had a car of his own when he was ten, a stripped Austin 7. When he was fifteen he moved up to a Morgan three-wheeler, beloved of two generations of British sports-car drivers. The Morgan had two wheels in front and a third, chain-driven, in the rear. The engine was usually a big motorcycle racing engine, and it rode out of doors, in front of the radiator. The Morgan was economically attractive because a whimsy of the law, concerning capacity and weight, classified it as a motorcycle, to its tax advantage; being light and over-powered, it had remarkable acceleration; also—and this was what brought a Morgan to Stirling Moss—one could legally drive a three-wheeled car before one could drive a four-wheeled one.

Moss's Morgan wasn't really a gift from his father. "My parents taught me," he has said, "that I could have what I wanted if I paid for it. I always managed to get what I was after, but in order to do that, I had to get rid of everything else. I could have a motorbike if I sold my radio and my chemical set and this and that and the other; and when I wanted to move on from the bike I had to flog off my tent and my camping kit and the bike itself and this and that. . . . I was taught that everything is attainable if you're prepared to give up, to sacrifice, to get it. I think my parents gave me, gave me as a gift, one might say, this belief, that what*ever* you want to do, you can do it if you want to do it enough, and I do believe that. I truly believe it.

"I believe that if I wanted to run a mile in four minutes I could do it. I would have to give up everything else in life, but I could run a mile in four minutes. I believe that if a man wanted to walk on water, and was prepared to give up everything else in life, he could do it. He could walk on water. I am serious. I really do practically believe that."

When Moss decided that he wanted to be a racing driver, his parents objected. His father argued on practical grounds: "*I* couldn't make a living at it, and I tried years ago, when it was easier."

They objected, but they didn't refuse. As former competition drivers they didn't think the *métier* as dangerous as parents without experience of it might, nor as unrewarding. They were outdoor people. They considered physical risk a natural part of life. After all, Stirling and Pat, five years younger, had been riding show horses and jumpers since they'd been old enough to say "horse" and no harm had come to them. So, after the Austin 7, the Morgan and the M.G. and such traditional school-cars of the British competition driver, Stirling graduated, at seventeen to a solid, reliable, medium-fast German sports car, a B.M.W. (*Bayrische Motoren Werke*) 328. In 1948, when he was eighteen and legally could drive in competition as well as on the roads, he got his first racing-car, a Cooper.

The Cooper, then (the firm is of course famous now), was made in a garage that has been described as approximately the size of a big kitchen. It was a Formula III car: 500 cubic centimetres of engine, which usually meant a rear-mounted one-cylinder J.A.P. or Norton racing motorcycle engine (the J.A.P. was a Morgan favourite, too) propelling it at speeds up to 105 miles an hour. The car was tiny and light. Steering was very quick and the engine delivered usable power only when it was turning fast: if speed dropped it would stall. The Cooper was a sprint and hill-climb car. Moss put in an entry for the famous Shelsley Walsh hill-climb. It was declined. Nobody had heard of him. He tried again, for a hill-climb at Prescott, the famous *venue* of the Bugatti Owners' Club. He was accepted, and on the scheduled day he loaded his Cooper into a horse-van and set off.

Prescott was then 880 yards of twisty, narrow road. Cars start on the flat, run over a rubber contact timing-device, scream up the hill and break an electric eye beam at the finish. Every major driver in Great Britain has run at Prescott. Moss's first assault on the hill was ragged. But each car is given two chances, and his second run was a record for the 500 c.c. class. It didn't last long, it was broken three times in the course of the day, but still, it's a fact:

The entire 1948 *equipe*: Stirling, his mother and his father.
The car is a Cooper 500.

H. R. Claytonr

Running hard through mountain country:
Moss in a Sunbeam Talbot in a Monte Carlo Rally.

At the top of the Futa Pass in the epic 1955 *Mille Miglia*:
Moss, Jenkinson, Mercedes-Benz.

A blessing from Guerrino Bertocchi, Maserati chief mechanic, just before *Mille Miglia*, '57.

Jesse L. Alexander

Spa, 1960: Moss has lost the left rear wheel of the Lotus, knows where he is going to hit, is spinning the car around.

The impact.

Jesse L. Alexander

Jesse L. Alexander

White spot at left is Moss's helmet, the Lotus is across the road; the other car is stopping.

Jesse L. Alexander

The Lotus afterward. Moss held the wheel as car hit.
At right: engine-cooling water line.

Stirling Moss broke a course record the first time he ran in competition (and the last time, too, if it comes to that). Knowledgeable people at Prescott that day, noting the speed with which he learned the hill, and seeing that he made no mistake twice, marked him as a novice to watch, and one perceptive journalist so cited him in print. The next time he ran in a hill-climb he won it. He entered an airport race and won that, in pouring rain. He went to the new Goodwood circuit and won there, in fast company. In all, in his first year, a boy, he entered fifteen events and won eleven of them.

For the next year's racing he bought a bigger Cooper, with a two-cylinder engine. He kept on winning. His father, reluctantly supporting his campaign, serving as his manager, conceded that there would be no return to the hotel business or any other so prosaic. With mixed feelings, he began to suspect greatness in his son. Moss was invited to run on the Continent, a small race at Lake Garda in Italy, and he was offered £50 in starting money. The Italians thought him amusing, a boy, a pink-cheeked Inglese with curly hair, and too much of it, then, as he has too little of it now. Some laughed at him and his funny-looking Cooper. He won his class, going away, set a lap record, and was an astonishing third overall to a pair of Ferraris, one of them driven by the formidable Luigi Villoresi. He went home with £200 in prize money. He began to believe in himself, to relax, to form his own style of driving, which is to say, properly, his own attitude toward the task at hand.

Much nonsense has been written about race-drivers' 'styles'. In an endeavour to give to the sport a complexity separate from, and additional to, those it does possess, the editors of motoring magazines like to run say three photographs of three cars in the same corner, picking three which show the drivers' hands in slightly different positions on the wheel. "These pictures of three notable stylists, all taken at the approach to Blindman's Bend, will reward careful study," the caption states. This is rubbish, of course. The pictures will reward careful study with eye-strain, and nothing more. Tennis-players, boxers, bull-fighters, *do* have varying methods and attacks that can be shown in still photographs, sometimes; but the distinctions of method that set race-drivers apart from one another are subtle, usually plain only to other drivers or to spectators standing close in selected locations, or in moving pictures—and that not often. The position of a driver's hands on the steering-wheel at ten to two or quarter to three is of little or no significance, and even this is becoming hard to see, since the bodywork of a *grand prix* car covers the driver almost to his chin.

(Another amusement is the standard photograph of two drivers in earnest conversation before a race. The caption, nine times in ten, will have them discussing 'strategy', whatever that is. I showed Stirling such a picture one day, asked him what he and the other fellow were really talking about. "Crumpet, what else?" he said.)

For many years steering systems of racing-cars were stiff and heavy; the muscular effort they required made the drivers sit close and work with bent arms; and the instability of the cars on the road necessitated numerous, rapid, almost continuous small movements of the steering-wheel. Cinema film made in the 1930's shows the drivers of such machines as the 500-horsepower Auto-Unions of Germany making continuous steering corrections whilst running dead straight! As steering geometries and road-holding improved, less movement of the wheel was required, and it became practical to sit well back from it. Nuvolari probably did it first, and then Farina. Neither moved as far back as Moss, who customarily drove with his arms very nearly straight out. Difficult to learn, and at first very awkward, the stance became almost universal as drivers learned that it conferred, in a way the old bent-arm attitude never could, a sense of control, balance and even serenity.

After the race at Lake Garda many drivers began to watch Stirling Moss and they saw, gladly or bitterly, as their natures ran, that he had the stamp of major talent; he seemed to be able to do things he had never been taught to do. Finally Tazio Nuvolari, the most revered figure in the sport, saw him and said to Basil Cardew of the London *Daily Express*: "Watch. He will be one of the great ones."

Since then Stirling has run in about 466 races, rallies, sprints, land-speed record attempts, endurance runs and so on. He has won 194 times! He has won forty-three per cent of all the races he has entered, a fantastically high percentage and one that no other driver has approached. For comparison, in another field, the American jockey, William Hartack, held to be one of the greatest, properly considered his 1957 season to be very successful. He won twenty-eight per cent of his races that year.

Moss has had much more than his share of mechanical break-downs, failures that have prevented his finishing, but he has finished 307 races in first, second, third or fourth places, and that is 65.8 per cent placements. The records set by Tazio Nuvolari, Rudolf Caracciola and Juan Manuel Fangio do not approach this record, except that Fangio, when he retired at the age of forty-eight, had won twenty-five races of the first category, while Moss had won fifteen when he was hurt at Goodwood. In 1961, the last full season he had, Moss started forty-eight events and won twenty-three of them. Of leading drivers who ran in international events in 1961, Jack Brabham entered sixteen events and won seven;

Jimmy Clark entered sixteen, won one; Graham Hill's ratio was 11:1; Phil Hill's was 9:4; McLaren, 18:0; Salvadori, 17:1; Surtees, 10:2; Moss entered twenty and won fifteen. In 1962, when he had won the Grand Prix of New Zealand in a spilling, solid, tropical downpour, and had lapped every man in the field to do it, including former world champion Jack Brabham, another driver said: "I wouldn't mind, if he was a human being!"

What kind of driving is this that Moss does, and the other fifteen or twenty men who are classified in any one year as drivers of *grand prix* stature? It is hard to understand because it relates to ordinary driving in about the same way as mountain-climbing relates to riding up a flight of stairs on an escalator. Basically the idea is to drive so fast that the car barely maintains adhesion to the road, runs just a hair this side of a tremendous slide and loss of all control. Richard Seaman, the brilliant British driver who was killed at Spa in Belgium in 1939, was probably first to say that driving a *grand prix* car on dry concrete produces exactly the same sensation as driving a fast sports car on a frozen lake. The fastest driver is the one who can come closest to the point at which the car's tyres will break adhesion to the road and let the machine go into an uncontrolled slide. ('Uncontrolled' is the key word. Much of the time, the driver has deliberately broken the car loose and is allowing it to slide, but under control.) Since the speed at which the driver will 'lose' the car varies with the individual machine, with the kind of tyres fitted and their state of wear, with the weather and the condition of the track surface, and may change every few hundred feet all around a 5.6-mile course, a fantastic degree of skill is required. A driver of Moss's ability, or near it, will decide in practice, for example, that the car will leave the road in a certain corner at ninety-seven miles an hour—

although he will not have this figure, or any miles-per-hour figure, in his mind. He will go through the corner in the race at, say, 96.5 miles an hour, over and over again, perhaps a hundred times. Other good drivers will go through at 95 one lap, 96.3 the next time and so on in a slightly varying pattern. Moss will beat them. Another will try the corner at 98. He will go off the road. This exercise is mildly complicated by the omission of a speedometer from the racing-car's intrument-panel; the information it gives is not precise enough. The driver judges car speed by feel, and by engine-speed, which is important: "You can take Red Horse Corner at 4,500 in third gear."

That is the basic skill required, to be able to estimate, almost instantaneously, and always accurately, that the four little oval patches of rubber that alone hold the car to the road, like a fly walking upside-down on a ceiling, will give up and let go of it here at 49 miles an hour, there at 103, there at 158, and, having made the estimation, to keep the car within a fraction of those speeds, steadily and consistently.

Next one must be able instantly to modify the entire equation in the event of rain, or sand or oil on the track. (*Grand Prix* racing is not stopped or slowed in the rain unless visibility comes down to zero, or there is flood-water on the circuit or something of that sort. Moss can recall only two such instances in his career.)

Next, one must be able to maintain speed in traffic, among cars going faster in some places and slower in others. One must learn such useful techniques as slip-streaming, placing a slow car directly behind a fast one, so that the low-pressure area, creating a vacuum effect, will give one a tow. If this is to work, one must be very close to the other car, sometimes within inches. In 1951, Moss forced Villoresi to tow him in this fashion for more than 90 miles! Aside from the obvious danger of collision at say 140 miles an hour, there are other risks: the exhaust of the car ahead can sicken a following driver; the wheels can throw sand into his engine, stones into radiator, windscreen, face.

One must be able to handle other little emergencies, such as coming around a corner to find another car spinning in front of one; or having a wheel break off; or having the car catch fire, or lose its clutch or its brakes. (Total loss of the clutch, making clutchless gear-changes imperative, or total loss of the brakes, should not stop a first-class driver. When Moss and William Lloyd won the Twelve Hour Race at Sebring, Florida, in 1954, Moss drove the last four hours or so, after nightfall, without the clutch and without a trace of braking-power. After the race, Moss asked a writer to get into the car and put the brakes on full; he then pushed it down the circuit at a dog-trot with one hand. During the race he had avoided a couple of stark emergencies by sliding the car sideways.)

Moss has not run in rallies in recent years (Pat Moss is one of the best women rally-drivers, three times Woman Champion of Europe), but he did earlier in his career.

"Some people would say I cheated, winning the Alpine the third time," he said, "but I didn't. That year, you had to do a speed test on a dead straight, a kilometre and a half or so. You had to make a certain minimum, I've forgotten what it was, but it was pretty high for the car I was driving, a Sunbeam Talbot saloon. Mike Hawthorn and Pete Collins were in the team.

"Before we came to the test I stopped and drained the oil from the engine, the gearbox, the back axle, the lot, and filled everything up with a very thin oil, really thin, practically the kind of stuff you'd use to lubricate a typewriter or a sewing machine. I blew the tyres up to about seventy-five pounds and I blanked off the whole of the radiator with cardboard to stop the air going in and getting bottled up under the bonnet. I made the speed I needed: Mike and Pete didn't.

"When we came to the end of the rally, I'd had trouble with the gearbox and I'd lost all but third. John Cutts, who was my co-driver, somehow managed to find second, just by *jamming* it in, so I had second and third for the special test; but somebody heard me changing gear and reported that I hadn't the gears, so a marshal was assigned to my car, to ride with me.

"Now, we had overdrive on those cars on all gears and that was working, so I started off in second, telling the marshal: 'Here's first gear,' then I took it out of second, waggled it around, diverted his attention, flipped the overdrive switch and stuffed it back into second.

" 'Oui,' the marshal said.

"Then I took it out and put it into the real third, the working one, and he said 'Oui' again and I said 'Oui' and then I took it out and waggled it around, hit the overdrive switch again, stuck it into third once more, said: 'Right, there's fourth,' and the marshal kindly said 'Oui' again and I was home and dry—except for running the test itself, of course, but I managed that all right."

The average speeds imposed by point-to-point rally organizers are often so high that the cars have to go flat out on some sections. The first seven cars to finish the 1963 Monte Carlo Rally were front-wheel drive cars, Saabs, Citroens, Mini-Minors, and one of the reasons for their success was evident in the technique of the Swedish driver Eric Carlsson, winner for the second year in succession. Approaching a right-hand corner, Carlsson would turn the steering-wheel to the right, keeping the front wheels under power, kick the brake-pedal with his left foot to lock the rear wheels for a split second, and send the car sliding into the corner, pointing straight through it and under full acceleration. To drive a car in such a fashion for 2,000 miles or so, hundreds of them over ice and snow-covered mountain roads, requires a formidable amount of skill. It's a matter of record that Moss once made up *twelve minutes going down-hill in the Alps.* Competent professional observers recorded their emotions while sitting in the back seat of a sedan Moss was driving at 78 miles an hour on black glare ice in the mountains. They were mixed.

"We're just as likely to go off the road at thirty as at eighty," Moss said, "so we may as well press on."

It is my belief that these skills, in their highest orders, are not available to men of normal physical equipment. Moss's physical equipment is demonstrably not normal. Like Joe Louis at his peak, when, he has said, he often found that he had hit a man before his brain had had time to note the opening, Moss has often braked, accelerated, or changed course before his brain could record the reason. He remembers braking an ordinary touring car so quickly in a road incident, that he was thrown forward on the seat—he hadn't had time to brace himself! His vision, before the Goodwood accident, was startlingly abnormal. Denis Jenkinson, one of the most reliable of observers in this field, tells of an occasion on which Moss identified a driver by name at a distance at which Jenkinson, who has normal corrected vision, could not be sure of the colour of the car. Moss's visual faculties were fantastic: he could change focus from say one mile to thirty inches to one mile almost instantaneously. His perception approached the extra-sensory: he could reduce his time over a 3-mile course by a second a lap; he could sense a gained or lost one-fifth second, going through a corner.

Up to Easter Monday 1962 at Goodwood, it was usually held that no one had seen Stirling Moss make a major error of judgement. Off the road enough to bash a wing on a hay-bale, yes, or run up on the kerb, that sort of thing, yes, but serious, no. No one knows what happened at Goodwood. Thousands saw the accident but no one knows what caused it, least of all Moss, who still has the amnesia typical of his injury. Driving a Lotus, he was in fourth place in the ninth lap when the gear-box stuck in fourth. He came in and the mechanics, inside five minutes, fixed the gearbox. Almost any stop will ruin a driver's chances in today's *grand prix* racing and when Moss went out again, he was three laps, or 7.2 miles, behind Graham Hill, leading. He had absolutely no chance of winning, but typically ("One's a race-driver or one's not"), he began to drive on the absolute limit. The year before, at the Zandvoort circuit in Holland, in a similar situation, with no chance at all of winning, he broke the lap record seven times. He broke the course record at Goodwood this time, too, and made up an entire lap, 2.4 miles. He came up behind Graham Hill, since become champion of the world, at around 120 miles an hour, out of a fast bend, Fordwater, into a slower one, St, Mary's. It is not a stretch in which drivers ordinarily attempt passing. Moss changed from fifth to fourth gear at the proper place, but at this point Graham Hill, watching his mirrors, was astounded to see that Moss's car was not slowing, but was coming on; observers saw him pull almost abreast of Hill's car and then go straight on 60 yards or so into an earth bank. Moss did slow the car down to something around 60–80 miles an hour before he hit, but he hit head-on, he did not spin the car, which would have been the logical, the standard thing to do.

The explanations were various: (1) He had finally made

a major error in judgement and was trying to overtake Hill at a point in the circuit where it couldn't be done. There is always a first time. The great Italian driver Achille Varzi never had a real accident until the one that killed him at Berne in 1948. (2) When Moss lifted his foot off the accelerator after shifting from fifth to fourth, the throttle stayed down. In the same car, the throttle had jammed the week before. (3) The engine had suddenly cut out. When this happens the car can go instantly out of control.

Laurence Pomeroy, a world authority on the racing car, was nearby. He considers that the behaviour of the car was typical of a throttle jammed wide open, and that Moss had one second, or one second and a half at the most, in which to assess the situation, decide what to do, and do it. Ordinarily that would have been time enough. Most of Moss's retirements have been due to mechanical failure. He can't remember how many times he has had to cope with steering failure, lost brakes, clutch, transmission, how many times he has run out of oil, water, petrol. He lost his chance in one race because when he hit the starter button he found the battery dead—in a car that had been two weeks in preparation!

"I can't believe the number of races that I've honestly seen thrown away by something really stupid!" he says.

Among the uninformed Moss has a reputation as a car-breaker. It is undeserved. The same was said of Nuvolari, who asked only that a car do what it had been designed and built to do. The ranking race-team manager of all time, Alfred Neubauer of Mercedes-Benz, for whom Moss drove in one of his two efforts in non-British cars, scoffs at the notion that Moss is hard on cars. So does Rob Walker, for whom Moss was driving when he had the Goodwood accident. So does Alf Francis, Moss's head mechanic for so many years: "It is uncanny how often Stirling is the

driver who first experiences a particular weakness [in a car].
It is not that he thrashes cars, because I know, better than
anyone else, that he does not."

Enzo Ferrari, whose experience in racing goes back farther
than anyone else's who is now active in the sport, is another
who does not care to hear it said that Moss is a car-breaker.

Had Moss been driving for Ferrari the past few years he
would have been champion of the world probably three
times. Instead, he drove British cars during the post-war
years when they were not really in the running, he drove
makes the names of which are today remembered only by
the enthusiast: Kieft, H.W.M., Alta, E.R.A. When British
grand prix cars, Lotus, Cooper and B.R.M. did begin to
demonstrate superiority over Continental machines, Moss
drove privately-owned models, always a year behind, a few
miles an hour slower, a shade harder to handle than the cars
in the factory teams.

The only legitimate professional criticism that can be made
of Moss is that he has not been a good judge of cars. He
will concede the point. He has picked the wrong cars either
because he didn't know they were the wrong ones, or because
they were British and privately-owned. He is fiercely
patriotic, even chauvinistic. "Everything else is a suburb
of London," he says, and he means it. Sometimes he talks
as Stirling Moss, racing driver, and sometimes as Stirling
Moss, O.B.E., who has taken cocktails with Her Majesty
the Queen and dined with the Prime Minister.

In 1951 Enzo Ferrari offered Moss a place in his team for
a race at Bari. When Moss appeared for practice the first
day he asked which was his car, and was told that he had
no car. Ferrari had changed his mind and, without notifica-
tion, had assigned Moss's car to the veteran Piero Taruffi.
Moss felt that he had been grossly maltreated and that,

through him, his country had been insulted. He announced, profanely, that Ferrari had seen the last of him.

For ten years and more Moss raced against Ferrari cars, and beat them when he could, which was often enough. But, toward the end of that time, in sports-car and touring-car (*gran turismo*) events, he began to drive Ferrari cars for private owners. Ferrari G.T. cars have been notably successful in long, hard races, like the 24-hour Le Mans, the 12-hour Sebring. They are strong, reliable, lasting, qualities attractive to Moss, who has had so many fragile horses shot out from under him.

Says Moss: "I can remember, off-hand, starting fourteen races in Ferrari motor-cars. In twelve, I finished. Once, I was disqualified, and once a fan-blade came off, after some twelve hours of running. Other than that—nothing. Man, a Ferrari will *really* stay together!"

Enzo Ferrari once drove. Later, when he was a team-manager, Tazio Nuvolari drove for him. He could not be indifferent to ability on the soaring level at which Moss operated. Nor could Moss withhold respect from a man the product of whose mind and hands came so near perfection. They are both realists. The climate around them began slowly to better, and in April of 1962, just before the Goodwood crash, Moss flew to Italy to see Ferrari. *Il Commendatore* sent a coupé to Milan for him to drive the hundred miles to the factory at Modena. Although he has been known to keep waiting for two hours a customer anxious to buy $50,000 worth of motor-car Ferrari came to greet Moss immediately. He showed him through the Ferrari factory, one of the industrial wonders of Italy and considerably harder to enter than the Vatican. He showed him the 1962 cars and —a gesture of rare trust—he showed him the drawings and plans for the 1963 cars. He gave him lunch and told him that he was as great a driver as Nuvolari had been, and greater than Fangio. He asked Moss to come to Italy and drive Ferrari cars. People who had long known Enzo Ferrari could not believe their ears when they were told of the conversation, which took place before George de Carvalho of *Time*.

"I need you," this harsh, imperious, gifted man said to Moss. "Tell me what kind of car you want and I will make it for you in six months. Put your ideas on paper for me. If you drive for me, you will tell me on Monday what you did not like about the car on Sunday and by Friday it will have been changed to your taste. . . . If you drive for me, I will have no team, just you and a reserve driver. With Moss, I would need no team. . . ."

"It must have shaken you," I said to Stirling.

"It did indeed," he said. "It was fantastic. Because Ferrari *could* make a new car in six months, you know. A British company might take two years, but he really could do it; and he could, and I think he would, change anything you wanted changed from Monday to Friday, as Mercedes-Benz would . . . but, I don't know, I think it would be anti-climactic, winning the world championship on an Italian car after all these years. . . ."

"He'd be world champion tomorrow if he'd sign with Ferrari," Ken Gregory, Moss's business manager, once said. "But he won't."

"I admit I like being the under-dog, coming from behind, doing things the hard way," Moss said.

Would he have gone to Ferrari if he hadn't been hurt at Goodwood? Will he go to Ferrari, should he ever race again? No, both times, I think.

Pulling him toward Ferrari would be the comparative ruggedness and reliability of Ferrari's cars—no matter how

resilient a man may be, no matter what reserves of spirit he
has to draw upon, it's hard to go to the rim of death and
stay there in suffering for weeks on end because a silly piece
of steel broke in two.

Too, the sheer richness of Ferrari's facilities would pull
Moss toward him. Except for his brief spells with Mercedes-
Benz and Maserati, Moss's racing has been done for small-
scale teams, hampered by shortages of cash, mechanics,
spares, transport and everything else that goes to make up
a major operation. With Ferrari, racing is first, and the
functions of all other operations are merely to support it.
Moss likes to travel first class. Himself a professional to the
bone, he cannot really admire anyone who is less, and he
knows that Enzo Ferrari's dedication to his life's work is
awesome.

How these two strong-minded men would get on together
is interesting to contemplate. Moss is as much a tycoon in
his way as Ferrari in his. *Il Commendatore* Ferrari could
not confer status upon Stirling Moss, O.B.E. To an extent
undreamt-of by drivers before him, Moss has made racing
a full-time business. His income from accessories and en-
dorsements alone is important. His ten-year contract with
British Petroleum Limited is a model of its kind. One reason
for the ferocity of his efforts to cure himself when he has
been hurt has been that he wanted to get back to the main-
stream of his life; but another was the simple fact that when
he's not driving a major source of his income stops. He is
not profligate and he is not penurious. He has a firm sense
of values. His father, and Ken Gregory, his friend for years
and his business manager, have shrewdly conserved and in-
vested his money, and he need not concern himself about
security for the rest of his life. He likes to live well. He
dresses carefully. He has the hipless, wide-shouldered build

that tailors like and in 1961 he was listed as one of the ten best-dressed men in Great Britain. He has some of his jackets made without pockets, so that he won't be tempted to carry anything that would spoil the line. His taste in food is pedestrian but his taste in restaurants is not. He moves among interesting people. When King Hussein of Jordan visited Prime Minister Macmillan and was asked whom he would like to have as a guest at dinner at 10 Downing Street he asked for Moss. ("A pleasant man," Stirling said of King Hussein. "Relaxing to be with. He makes an impression of great courage.") When he is in London Moss entertains often. His house in the West End, more than two years in building, is as nearly finished now as anything belonging to an obsessive perfectionist can be, and Moss designed it as much for entertaining as for his own comfort.

This is, I suppose, the most electrified, most automated private dwelling in London. I once threatened Stirling, in mock anger, that if he didn't do something I wanted done, I would pull the main fuse in his house.

"You know what that means, mate," I said to him. "You won't be able to open a closet door to get a clean shirt. The drapes won't work. Worst of all—a stone-cold toilet seat!"

There are two ordinary things about the Moss house. It is on a street and it has a number. But there comparison pretty well ends. Everything else about it from basement to roof is unique: it stands on a bomb site that was the only piece of freehold land Moss could find for sale in the entire West End, and its television aerial is not on its own roof, it's on the roof of the new Hilton Hotel—or soon will be.

Moss designed the five-floor building himself. He has a vivid imagination and he did not spare it. He has visited elegant and modern homes from Bangkok to Berlin, and when he saw an idea he liked, he remembered it. And he had the place put together properly. The contractors came to know that if Moss saw a bit of cracked paint on a window-sill, the phone was going to ring two minutes later.

Behind a large plate-glass window on the ground floor is the reception room of Moss's office. His private office is behind it. There are two doors from the street, one on the left leading to the office, the other in the centre right to the house. A hidden television camera is trained on the house-door. When the bell rings, a flick of a master-switch will cut out whatever programme is on the television, cut in a closed circuit and project the caller. The garage door runs on a sonic system: an ultra-high whistle, held in the hand like a bulb-horn, or operated electrically from a car, will open or close the doors from thirty yards away. Inside the garage, a door leads into the central hallway of the building, as does the front door proper. Another door leads to Moss's private office, but this door is concealed in the wall, knobless, hung on buried hinges. A circular staircase tightly wound inside a plastered steel tube, the steps red-carpeted, leads up and down: down to a conference room panelled in driftwood, the housekeeper's quarters, the oil-fired furnace for the ducted hot air central heating. The air-conditioning plant is in the basement, too: in warm weather it will cool the air throughout the house, and at all times it filters it. This is not an ordinary house air-conditioning unit: it functions to industrial/hospital standards.

The rear wall of Moss's private office is a sheet of plate glass, looking out on a tiny garden, a rock-wall, a pool and a fountain. His desk is a long, angled piece of rosewood and mahogany. The chairs are of teak and black leather. Glass-fronted bookcases hold two or three extraordinary model cars, a racing Talbot powered by a model aircraft engine, a G.P. Lotus carrying Moss's 7 and detailed down to working

suspension, steering, and detachable body-panels. There's a
Roy Nockolds painting, Moss in a bend in the Nurburg Ring
in this same Lotus; another, by M. D. H. Keane, a startled-
looking, doe-eyed blonde. High on the wall over a filing-
case are two 14-inch red-rimmed Lotus steering wheels, bent
and twisted by the terrible forces put through them when
Moss locked his hands on them at Spa and at Goodwood.

One wall of the outer office is papered with a photographic
enlargement of a detailed street-map of Moss's favourite
city, London. A magazine rack for visitors' use carries an
injunction: the magazines should not be carried away.

There are two rooms on the first floor, but they have the
effect of four: kitchen, living-room, dining-room, bar. The
ultra-modern kitchen might have been lifted intact out of
an American house in Westchester County or the Big Sur;
the bar has a photo-mural of New York's lighted skyline,
and both these things amused me when I saw them first;
Stirling says that he can't understand America. Occasionally
I want to remind him that his grandfather made a lot of
money in America, but I never have because it would have
nothing to do with the argument. Pinned to the wall, he
will say specifically only that he thinks New Yorkers are
rude and American policemen less ethical, to state it gently,
than British. We have had some lively discussions on these
points.

"Admit it, now," Moss says, "who're the politest people
you've known? The French? The Swedes? The Mexicans?
Who?"

"Taken by and large, the British," I said.

"Right. And where will you find anybody ruder than a
New York subway guard?"

"Nowhere," I said. "But as between a really nasty New
York subway guard and a casual selection among the British

upper classes, there's nothing in it. For example, so-and-so and so-and-so and so-and-so."

"So-and-so's a clot," Stirling said. "Just a wealthy clot, and nothing to do with the British aristocracy. I know the incident you're thinking of, and I'm surprised you didn't hit him."

"And the other two?"

"I would say they're not typical."

"Neither's your New York subway guard, perhaps. I used to know one who spent his time off taking care of sick birds —birds with wings, I mean."

"There'll be pigeon pie tonight!" Stirling said. "I know —and New York cops are always delivering babies in patrol cars. Is it true they have to take a course in obstetrics before they can get on the force?"

"In New York, yes—but not the ones you've had trouble with, in Georgia and Florida and so on."

"Do you know I've had a Florida cop start to pull his gun on me?" Stirling said. "Can you imagine a London bobby doing that—if he *had* a gun, that is?"

"No," I said. "But if you brought that Florida state trooper to London and put him on a beat in Marylebone and he saw how much respect he got from the people, and that he was safe as churches, totally unarmed, his attitude would change; and the bobby from Chelsea, working in Florida, if he heard that one of his mates had got half his head blown off without warning, asking a man for his driver's licence—well, *his* attitude would change, too."

"Life in the jungle," Stirling said.

"Never mind," I said. "Tell me about this oven—does it cook with gas, electricity, infra-red rays, atomic energy, or what?"

"With plain old electricity," he said.

Nothing else is plain about the kitchen. A hotel-style hood over the range, equipped with exhaust blowers, takes care of cooking smells. The sink and working surfaces are stainless steel, and everywhere are odd little Moss touches: the bread-drawer has a sliding top that makes a cutting surface; if crusts are trimmed to make toast, for example, a slot opens to receive them. Cabinet doors, equipped with push locks that open at a touch, swing out and their shelves swing out, revealing yet other shelves that swing out in their own turn. Garbage disposal is mechanical, of course: the stuff is pulped and flushed down the drain. There's a break-fast-nook, a serving window connecting with the dining area, and a service lift connects all floors so that food can quickly be sent anywhere in the house.

Facing the front of the house is the living room, with a dining area at one end. This is a long room, a high window running almost the length of it, with curtains running along an aluminium track under electric power. The motor is controlled from one of the switch-plates on the wall just inside the door. Every light-switch in the house is a touch-button, by the way; there are no old-fashioned clickers.

The heavy curtains are deep green; the thick, cushioned rug is green; the walls are white. Most of the furniture is upholstered in rust-orange, most of the wood is teak, Moss's favourite. The furniture is either simple and straightforward, in the sound Scandinavian mould, or it is Chinese in deriva-tion. Moss has been no slave to consistency: the dining table is a slab of hammered glass six feet long and an inch thick, as modern as tomorrow, or the day after (there are two coffee-tables in the same glass), but in the other corner of the room, hovering low over a chess table, is a brass 18th-century post-lantern, tremendous, so big that at first it looks grotesque, and then, later on, reveals itself as quite right. The dining table, on the other hand, is lighted by a cluster of irregularly suspended ceiling lamps, and there are separate lights to illuminate two haunting South Sea portraits, painted on velvet and framed behind non-reflecting glass.

The wall at the other end of the room, behind a long, severely modern divan, is covered in rectangles of cork. A table at one end holds a telephone and intercom controls. Past this, and two small steps down, is the bar and dance floor; the ceiling is covered in black leather pierced by irregularly placed lights, with rheostat control from a red glow to full white brilliance. A teakwood cabinet, elaborately carved in the Chinese fashion, holds drinks, glasses, ice.

Up the winding stairs, steep enough and tight enough, nearly, for a light-house, there are two bedrooms and two bathrooms. One of the bedrooms is medium in size, the other is a big one. The smaller is the guest-room. Until recently, because the amount of electrical work involved in the master bedroom was delaying its completion, Moss slept in the guest-room, in a jumble of clothes, radios, magazines, odds and ends. Only two things were consistently in the room: his ten British Racing Drivers' Club gold stars, framed, and two large portrait photographs of his former wife, Katie Molson.

The master bedroom is finished now. It is spectacular. It's hard to know where to look first, although I think that for most people it would be a dead heat between the cherry-red fur bedspread—rabbit-skins raised on the Moss farm in Tring—and the big television set suspended on white cords from the ceiling. It doesn't *stay* jammed tight against the ceiling, of course: some of the buttons on the elaborate control-console at the head of the bed lower it, adjust it for viewing angle, turn it on, correct brightness and volume, turn it off and pull it back up again. There are controls for the hi-fi system as well, for the lights throughout the house, the doors, the closed-circuit television, telephones—and the tub in the master bathroom, push-button filled.

The bed itself is oversize, basically a rectangle, but wider at the head than at the foot. The effect is oddly pleasing, and has the practical value of leaving ample space for the gadgets Moss wanted built into the headboard area: cupboards, drawers, a small refrigerator and so on. There are three windows. They light a desk running the length of the room. Green-yellow grass-cloth fabric covers the walls.

One wall of the room is solid cupboard-space closed in by electrically-powered doors. When they are opened up the doors reveal an ample wardrobe—all of it cut and tailored to fit one not very tall but very demanding individual. Jackets hang on shaped hangers; oddments such as shirts and socks are in glass-fronted drawers; trousers hang, knife-edged, in a separate cupboard. There's a 'silent valet,' the usual thing designed to hold, overnight, a jacket, a pair of trousers, a pair of shoes, watch, change, wallet and so on. This one is different. There is a thermostatically-controlled heating-unit in it, it will *press* a pair of trousers overnight.

In an alcove off the cupboard area, facing a big mirror, there are twin wash-basins, and past them the bathroom, with shower, bidet, the big primrose-yellow, sunken free-form tub. A discreet glow of light signifies the working of the electric warming-circuit built into the toilet-set. The guest bathroom is ordinary by comparison, not more luxurious than one expects to find in a *de luxe* hotel.

Climbing the red spiral staircase once more, we come to the top—a bubble of glass lighting it—and a part of the Moss house planned solely for entertaining: a medium-sized room, a separate bar, a balcony. On two sides, walnut display cases will hold a selection, a few, of the hundreds of cups and trophies that Moss has won since he was first hoisted on to the back of a show-horse when he was six. The bar is a mass of teak. There's a refrigerator, of course, a teakwood cover conceals a small stove, a teakwood door opens on storage-space. The turn-table and the master controls for the hi-fi system—there are speakers throughout the house—are built into one wall of the trophy-room, and full-length glass doors open to the railed balcony.

It's an exciting house, exciting for many reasons; it would be exciting if one were taken through it by an estate-agent, without the least idea who'd built it, who owned and lived in it. But, knowing, it's the more exciting, I'm sure because it faithfully reflects Stirling Moss; it's a portrait of him, almost: a small house, tightly put together, jumping with ideas, and burning almost enough energy every day to run a train from London to Manchester—and halfway back!

CHAPTER II

"They can compare the call of the hills to the
melody of wonderful music, and the comparison
is not ridiculous."

G. H. Leigh-Mallory

CHAPTER II

WHEN I was writing this book, I had a note from Stirling, who was in Tokyo. At the bottom, under his signature, he had written: "What do you know about levitation?" This is typical of his curiosity. One day he told me how he had discovered, riding a bicycle in South Africa nine months after the Goodwood accident, that the left side of his body was still badly affected, because he could ride very well with both hands, with no hands, with his right hand only—but not at all with his left hand only. This led him to wonder what was the fastest a bicycle had been ridden, something which I knew—128 miles an hour—and that brought him to the whole matter of bicycles and how badly they were usually made, and what did *grand prix* cyclists of the old days do with steaks besides eat them. (They sat on them, because they helped prevent boils, an occupational hazard for racing cyclists.) When I left him that day, Stirling was on the point of designing a new bicycle. (And not for kicks, or *pour le sport,* either: he had been on the telephone to a Midlands works; money had been mentioned.)

A man so curious about everything around him, and so introspective and introverted as Moss is, might expect to be tortured by knowing that a career, perhaps just rising to a peak, had been terminated inside two seconds of time, five ticks of a watch—and that he didn't know why. Certainly he has been tortured, obviously he must have been, although he has never said so. I think that no accomplishment, no event, nothing in the man's life has been so remarkable, so stunning, even, as the fact that from the day he recovered consciousness to this minute, I have not heard that he has expressed the least regret. I have not heard him say, even, that it was a bad break; that he wished it might not have happened, or: "If I hadn't had the shunt at Goodwood." He has been perfectly tranquil about it, and, I think, in balance. A psychiatrist who had been trying to help Stirling over the misery of his broken marriage, before the crash, said, seeing him afterwards: "The man has matured ten years."

The only reference he has repeatedly made to the crash, to me, is that his being so close to death this time has, in some fashion he doesn't understand, heightened his appreciation of ethical behaviour.

"I've always tried to be honest in my own life," he says, "but since the accident I must admit that honesty has become an obsession with me. Not only in myself. In others. Unethical behaviour that I would have overlooked before, now makes me extremely angry. I don't know why I get so angry about any kind of dishonesty now, but I do, I just can't tolerate it."

That aside, there is the other thing: underneath it all, there is, because there must be, a burning wonder about Goodwood—what *did* happen?

I suggested to him that he have himself put into hypnosis, when he was well enough to stand the shock of going through the accident again, and see if he could find out in that way. Andrew Salter of New York is an eminent authority in this field, and my friend; I phoned him to ask if he thought this would be feasible. Of course, he said—providing that Stirling had *known,* at the time, what was happening. He might not have been able to determine, in his second and a half, what was taking the car off the circuit. If he did know, the information was there, buried under the protective amnesia, and he could recall it in hypnosis. Unhappily, Salter reminded me, the paralysis complicated matters. Taken back through the accident, Moss might suffer paralysis again, in the involuntary hysterical form, and it might or it might not be easy to remove it. I would think the risk too great, even though Stirling is familiar with hypnosis, because he was curious about it some years ago, and because his father has used it in dentistry.

If he does decide to chance the procedure, and it is successful, I think he will recall that the symptoms preceding the accident were those of a jammed throttle. Ken Gregory, on the basis of a careful, prolonged, inch-by-inch examination of the car, says that the throttle cannot have stuck. We disagree. The weight of authority and experience is on his side, but I think that no examination of a car that has been through a sixty-mile-an-hour head-on crash could demonstrate that the throttle had *not* stuck. But perhaps it didn't. Whatever the cause, logic argues that it was some kind of mechanical fault, because nothing in Stirling's past, nothing in his behaviour that day, would account for his losing the car in those circumstances. If that thesis could be demonstrated, he would be glad, because he could then still say that he has never had an accident that wasn't caused either by someone else or by something breaking on the car. But he would be depressed, too, that he wasn't able, in that second and a half, to do more about it. He has done more, other times and other places.

For example, in 1957 he started the *Mille Miglia,* the Thousand Miles open-road race in Italy, abandoned since that year, the year that Portago was killed. Moss started in a big Maserati, the last car to leave the line at Brescia for the run to Rome and back. With him was Denis Jenkinson, his navigator in the 1955 *Mille Miglia,* which they won at the all-time record average speed of 97.7 miles per hour. They had barely started, they were only a few miles out, when they had what Moss calls not an accident but an incident: the brake-pedal shaft broke in half. He told me about it in a letter a few days later:

". . . I was approaching the corner at approximately 130 miles an hour in fifth gear. I estimated that the corner could be taken at about 90–100, therefore it was a fairly sharpish curve, to the left. I lifted my foot off the accelerator and put it on the brake, and, on increasing pressure on the pedal it suddenly shot forward and broke off. More or less at the same time I was dropping the car down into fourth gear. I pulled the handbrake on, which was useless; pushed the car into third gear, immediately followed by second. I remember the car fish-tailing a little. At the same time as all this I attempted to put the car into a bit of a broadside to lose a little speed. I managed to get the car around the corner and then dropped it into first gear. Finally Denis Jenkinson and I had to jump out and stop it manually! When I tell you there were absolutely no brakes at all it is not an exaggeration. . . ."

That is how Moss considers an emergency should be managed. He had pulled the car down from 130 miles an hour to two or three miles an hour, in a brutally short distance, without enough braking power to stop a child's tricycle, and he had done it in a corner and on a narrow road. On a closed circuit, with room in which to cope with emergencies, he would probably have kicked the pedal to one side and gone on without brakes.

He and Jenkinson turned the car around by hand, so as not to let it roll into the ditch, and roared back to Brescia.

Moss came out of the car in a rage, waving the broken pedal over his head, but he couldn't maintain his anger in the face of the horror and humiliation of the Maserati *équipe*. There was talk of sabotage, but it wasn't true. The pedal shaft had been made of a flawed piece of metal.

Moss was the more annoyed because he would like to have topped his running of the 1955 *Mille Miglia* for Mercedes-Benz, a classic performance, one of the greatest motor-races ever run. Not only that, it was probably the best-reported motoring performance of all time, because Denis Jenkinson, Moss's co-driver, is uniquely equipped as a journalist. An ex-motorcycle side-car champion of the world, he is tranquil at any speed. Riding passenger on a racing motorcycle, leaping about from side to side to balance the rig, hanging out with one's chin three inches from the concrete, will make a man tranquil or mad or dead in short order. Jenkinson is also an authority on the behaviour of the motor-car at high speed, knows exactly what is happening at all times, and is an excellent writer as well.

Moss had asked Jenkinson if he would try the race because he believed that with someone of Jenkinson's intelligence and ice-cold temperament it might be possible for a non-Italian team to win the race. The *Mille Miglia* was held to be an Italian monopoly, because it was thought that no one other than an Italian could hope to learn the road. (Moss was the first Englishman ever to win it, and the second non-Italian. Caracciola won it in 1931.) In really high-speed driving it's no use to come around a corner and look to see if the road goes straight, or right, or left. If you don't know which way the road goes *before* you see it, you will be absurdly slow or you will crash, and there is no other alternative. Really hurrying, it is sometimes necessary to go through a right-hand bend with the car pointing to the left. An

Italian like Piero Taruffi, who won in 1957, having driven Brescia—Rome—Brescia scores of times in his fifty-four years, *knew* which way the road went. He was also a famous mountain-driver. Moss realized that neither he nor Jenkinson nor any other Englishman could memorize a thousand miles of Italian road—but he thought it might be possible to plot or map a thousand miles of road, if he could find a man cold enough to sit beside him, read the map, and *tell* him, before every curve, every blind hill-brow, every bridge, which way the road went afterward.

Moss and Jenkinson ran the course in practice again and again, smashed two cars (one of them against an Italian army truck full of live ammunition) and put the whole route down on a strip of paper seventeen feet long, rolled into a plastic case. They made up a set of hand signals, since the Mercedes-Benz 300 SLR they were running was an open car and conversation would be impossible over engine-noise and wind-roar. A signal might mean: "Right-hand bend, flat-out in third gear, straight afterward." By constant reference to mile-posts, bridges, churches, even brightly-coloured houses, Jenkinson really navigated the car—he knew to within a few yards where they were at any given moment. In practice, Moss developed so much confidence in Jenkinson that he could, in the race, accept Jenkinson's signal that the road went straight after a blind brow ahead; he could hold his foot flat on the floor, go over the crest at 170 miles an hour, let the car fly for fifty yards, and press on. They went into *cities* at 125–150 miles an hour! It was nine-tenths and ten-tenths motoring, absolutely flat out, nothing left. Jenkinson told of their passing low-flying aeroplanes; of Moss, going down a steep hill flat out in third gear, shifting to fourth and standing on the accelerator-pedal. "It took a brave man to do that. . . ." he wrote later. Jenkinson was

burned by the hot gear-box; the G-forces in the turns made
him vomit; he lost his glasses overboard in the slip-stream,
but in 10 hours, 7 minutes and 48 seconds of the fastest over-
the-road motoring anyone has done since the motor-car was
invented, he made not one mistake and missed giving only
one signal, when a full tank sloshed a pint of petrol down
his back. Afterward he found it extremely difficult to express
his admiration for Moss's mastery of one of the fastest cars
in existence over open road running the length and breadth
of Italy. In a letter to me after he had read a magazine
article I had done about Moss, Denis Jenkinson wrote:
". . . I too think that Moss is the greatest driver, and a
genius. . . ."

As for Moss, he said: "I might have finished the race without Denis Jenkinson, although I doubt it, but I couldn't
possibly have won without him." (Later he said to me: "An
interesting thing, Denis told me that because he knew that he
could not handle a 300 SLR at that speed, that it was beyond
him and foreign to his experience, he wasn't frightened; but
that had I been driving a Porsche, which he knows, and
which he can drive very well himself, then he'd have been
badly frightened. As for me, no amount of money, nothing,
would persuade me to sit for 10 hours in a car that somebody
else was driving at 170 miles an hour over blind brows. The
very thought of it frightens me!")

Moss went to the celebration dinner in Brescia. Then,
noticing that he wasn't really tired (the effect of caffeine
tablets he'd taken before the race coupled with his own
adrenal output) he got into his own car and drove to Stutt-
gart, and on from there to Cologne, where he took a plane
to England. It was a fantastic end to a fantastic day. He
had more than justified Alfred Neubauer's faith in him. In
1954, driving his own Maserati, Moss was beating Fangio,

on a factory Mercedes-Benz, when an oil-line broke. He pushed the car a half mile to the finish-line. Said Neubauer: "That refusal to give up impressed me almost as much as his magnificent driving."

In Germany, in 1961, he had another legendary triumph: he won the German Grand Prix on the Nurburg Ring in a car that was twenty miles an hour slower than the favoured Ferrari. The 'Ring,' in the Black Mountains, is one of the most difficult of circuits, 14.2 miles to the lap, with up- and down-hill grades as high as 1 in 5, and 187 bends and corners —or more, or less, depending upon who has last counted them. It is a 'driver's circuit,' which is to say that the driver is more important than the car; skill counts most on the Nurburg Ring. Courage enough to put the foot flat to the floor can never be decisive, although you won't win without it. A virtuoso can do wonders on the Ring. In 1935 Tazio Nuvolari beat the combined Mercedes-Benz and Auto-Union teams of Germany, held to be unconquerable except by each other, and he beat them in an aging Alfa-Romeo that was twenty miles an hour slower than they were. Moss's 1961 run, in an obsolescent, outmoded, privately-owned Lotus running against Phil Hill, champion of the world, leading the factory-entered Ferraris, was the first to be seriously compared with Nuvolari's victory of twenty-five years before. Moss beat the Ferrari team by 21.4 seconds, which is a long time, a very long time, as *grand prix* racing goes today.

The car he used was the same Lotus with which he had won the 1961 *Grand Prix* of Monaco earlier in the season, another race which is certain to be studied as long as the records are kept, a classic. Again, he did it on a driver's circuit: the Monaco G.P. is run through the streets of Monte Carlo. The knife-edge corners of marble buildings, glass shop-fronts, trees, the deep water of the harbour all wait for the driver to make one small mistake. The great Alberto Ascari, killed at Monza in 1955, was one whom the stand-by frogmen had to pull from the waters of the harbour. In 1962, the trees killed one driver and flying debris from another crash killed a track official. Top speed at Monaco is lower than on some courses, but only *virtuosi* can do a hundred really fast laps through the streets of Monte Carlo.

"To go flat-out through a bend that is surrounded by level lawn is one thing," Moss has said, "but to go flat-out through a bend that has a stone wall on one side and a precipice on the other—that's an *achievement*!"

"In 1961 at Monte Carlo," Moss told me, speaking in what was for him an oddly slow and sober fashion, "I was absolutely flat-out *at my own rating*. That is very unusual. Other people, even other drivers, may say: 'Well, old Moss was flat-out coming through such-and-such bend' and perhaps I was and perhaps what they took to be ten-tenths I reckoned was only eight-tenths. But at Monaco in 1961 I was on the limit. One doesn't very often run a race flat-out —ten-tenths. Nine-tenths, yes. But at Monte Carlo every corner, every lap as far as I remember, I was trying to drive the fastest I possibly could, to within a hair's-breadth of the limit, for at least 92 of the 100 laps. Driving like that is tremendously tiring, just tremendously tiring, most people have no idea what it does to one."

Some drivers consider a three-hour race the equivalent of a 60-minute football game; on a hot day cockpit temperatures may rise above 150° F.; a man may lose five to eight pounds in weight; on some confined circuits (Monte Carlo is one) crash-causing carbon monoxide poisoning from the car just ahead is a real danger. Some drivers pour water over themselves just before the start on a really hot day.

Says Moss: "I tried that, and of course it kept one cool for the first two or three laps, the least important of the race. It did no good at the end, when things really got hot. But for a long time I kept on doing it anyway, out of vanity! The other fellows started to copy me, they thought I found it cooling, but I was doing it for a different reason: I liked the way I looked in soaking wet overalls!"

Three-quarters of the way through the 1961 Monte Carlo race, Phil Hill, lying second, signalled the Ferrari No. 2 man, Richie Ginther, running behind him, to take up the attack on Moss. Ginther, a tiger, drove the race of his life, but Moss beat him by three seconds and a bit. The Monte Carlo crowd, sophisticated in motor-racing, was hysterical; the knowledgeable people in the pits, knowing Moss was doing something that really could not be done, were transfixed. Rob Walker, who owned the car Moss was driving, and who used to drive as an amateur, said:

"The last few laps I stopped watching; I couldn't look any more, I couldn't stand it."

On a course with long straights, the Ferrari drivers would simply have flattened their accelerators and let the superior power and speed of their cars overwhelm Moss; but on a street-circuit, up-hill-and-down, full of hairpins and right angles, with a curving tunnel that has daunted some brave men and deceived some good ones, that's a different matter. A driver changes gears 1400 or 1500 times doing the Monaco G.P. There is room for virtuosity to show itself.

In 1962, Moss didn't run at Monte Carlo. He watched the race on television in his room in the Atkinson Morley Hospital. There were the last few laps to run, and Phil Hill was increasing his speed fantastically in an attempt to catch Bruce McLaren, winning, when the B.B.C. shut the programme off in order to accommodate a serial. Moss was furious, but his primary concern, characteristically, was to get a radio going in time to hear the end of the broadcast. He has a curiously equable temperament for one so volatile. Motor-racing sometimes makes short tempers. I have seen wrenches thrown, and I've heard a driver screaming: "I'll kill the bastard!" while three mechanics struggled to hold him. Jean Behra, killed at Avus in 1959, once hit a Ferrari team manager, but Moss has never gone past the gesture of fist-waving, which is merely a convention, at a driver who balks his passing. He has done some boxing and some judo-playing, and with his quick strength and freakish reaction-time he'd have been murderous at either, but he hasn't had a fight since he was a boy at school. He is not often rude, but he can be, and when he feels that he must defend himself with a short answer, he always has one ready. Typically, since he never does anything without planning to do it, he is prepared to defend a rude action.

Driving across London early one morning recently, he passed another car on the wrong side. It was very early, there was not much traffic in the streets. A few minutes later, Moss was surprised to be stopped by a policeman. The officer and Moss had an amicable enough discussion about passing methods, there was no ticket, and when they were parting, Moss noticed, going by, the car he'd overtaken. He asked the policeman if, by any chance, the man in that car had complained. The answer was, yes. A few blocks farther on, and by no chance, Moss pulled up beside the fellow at some traffic lights. He hopped out of his car and ran over. The other man, considering that he was about to be assaulted, ran up his window, but he'd forgotten to lock the door. Moss pulled it open and thrust a pound note in at him.

"Here," he said, "take this, and for God's sake go and get a driving lesson, even if it's just one."

Stirling and I had an argument about the incident. I told him I thought he'd been brutally rude. "After all," I said, "it was an abuse of your position. It's as if Sonny Liston had punched a waiter, let's say. You shouldn't have done it."

"You're dead wrong!" Stirling said. "I should have done it, and I'll do it again. The fellow was a clot. He hadn't been hurt. He hadn't even been annoyed. He had no right to run looking for a bobby to set on me. I'd do it again, this instant."

"Do you suppose he knew who you were?" I asked, giving up the argument as one I was most unlikely to win.

"I don't know," Stirling said. "But he got someone to give me the pound back." He laughed.

Bone-deep toughness and a curious tendency to return to dead-centre egotism have marked every man and woman I've known who had accomplished much, or who had come anywhere near the aura of greatness, whether statesman, artist, writer, film producer or whatever. Moss is of this pattern, as he must be, and differs only in demonstrating less overt ego and more humility than any other great accomplisher I've known. I remember saying to a bullfighter, years ago, before I knew better: "You are the most egotistical bastard I've ever met."

He said: "You don't understand. When I go in there, if I don't really and truly believe I *am* the best in the world, I had better not go in at all."

That is part of it, that and the obsession. Everyone who accomplishes greatly is obsessed with one purpose and nearly blind to all else; he can only with difficulty tear his mind away from the one thing that is important to him to consider lesser matters—and everything except his purpose in life is a lesser matter. In the light of the obsession I know he has had to live with, I am inclined to marvel at Moss's gaiety every time I see him. I know very well he forces much of it, but still, it's there.

Rude he may be when he's crossed, but basically, I find him a courteous and considerate man. I could think of a dozen examples. Shortly after he was released from hospital, the first time, before the operations, some friends of mine from the United States, television people, came to London to make a film that was to be built around him. I went with them to Stirling's house one day, bringing my 11-year-old daughter, Tabitha, who had a monumental crush on him. Stirling was shaky that day. He was still unco-ordinated, he had to think out and shape each step he took, each move he made; it was hard for him to keep up an appearance of normal movement. He could not focus his left eye, he saw everything double, and the action planned for the film required him to drive a new M.G. through the narrow streets of Shepherd's Market and then through traffic in Knightsbridge, although he had done almost no driving since the accident. In his condition, most men would have done well to avoid being jumpy and bemused.

Still, when he saw Tabitha he thanked her for a letter she had written to him from Belgium when he was in hospital; twice, during interruptions in the shooting, he had earnest discussions with her on such urgent matters as the merits of the twist and the Madison, he posed for a picture with her, he waved to her when he passed in the M.G. (his chore at the wheel complicated by the tendency of motorists who recognized him to stand on the brake and point with both hands) and when we left he made a particular effort to say good-bye to the child. Right, if I had been a reporter Stirling had met that morning for the first time . . . after all, a successful public relations policy requires effort. But we were in the tenth year of our acquaintance. None of it was for me.

I have a mild compulsion about being on time for appointments and I amuse myself, when I have an appointment with Stirling, by being as nearly exactly on time as I can manage. He is unfailingly punctual, and he is the only person I know who truly appreciates punctuality. Just before the Goodwood crash I had an appointment with him for four o'clock one afternoon. I have an accurate watch, and I opened the door of his office five seconds before 4 o'clock. He looked at his own watch. "God, that's wonderful!" he said. "You're spot-on time!" He was more pleased than he'd have been with a present. We went to the garage and got into his yellow Lotus *Elite*. I asked him how he liked it.

"There's nothing to touch it," he said. "There is no other motor-car I know of, this side of a racing-car, that handles like an *Elite*. Coming back from Snetterton the other day I *averaged* sixty without ever going over seventy, and I think that's remarkable. It's the best thing of its kind in the world."

We ran out into the traffic of Park Lane. Stirling drove fast, but not conspicuously or spectacularly so, there was nothing remarkable about his driving except the machine-like precision of his gear-changing. (He prefers automatic transmission in his personal transport, and the Moss *Elite* now has a Hobbs unit.) It was like riding with any other professional. In the ordinary way of things, one should not expect anything remarkable to appear in his driving short of a hundred miles an hour or so, and not much then, this side of emergency. It would be in the country between 125 and 165 that there would be wonders to see, and only Denis Jenkinson has been there with him. I looked into cars beside us. It was remarkable, I thought, how many people recognized him and showed it.

A couple of girls in a Mini ran up beside us and looked in and smiled. "Crumpet to port," I said.

"I see," he said. We smiled at them. "The one driving is nice," Moss said. He let them pass and in the next block repassed them. If he had stopped, I suspect they'd have pulled up, too. Moss's effect on many women—some suspect too big an ego and dislike him on sight—demonstrates no technique, but derives from his brute energy—and of course from his position, his eminence—from his lively interest in everything going on around him, and his civility. He is essentially kind. In 1961 he saw on television a man who was paralysed and who needed a small van. Moss bought one, had it fitted for him and delivered, in the strictest secrecy. Nothing was known of it until the story leaked out following the Goodwood accident. Also after the accident two brief letters from spectators appeared in a motoring magazine, remarking that before the race began, a time that finds most drivers edgy, Moss had taken a man in a wheel-chair on a 30-minute tour of the paddock area to show him the cars; and had taken someone else, similarly immobile, on a tour of the circuit in a car, pointing out the various corners so that the announcer's comments would be the more graphic during the race. He then found the man a good vantage point and took him to it.

I think that not all of the motivation for these acts was so simple a thing as kindness, although it was kind behaviour indeed. But I believe that subconsciously Moss feels a kinship with handicapped people and somehow identifies himself with them. Perhaps it has something to do with his realization that a racing-driver knows, every time he gets into his car, that before the afternoon is out, he may know four sensations in quick succession: joy, with the car running like a rocket under a hot blue sky; shock, with the realization that something's suddenly gone terribly wrong; bewilderment, as the brain tries, inside the fat part of a second, to sort out the impressions pouring into it and decide what is happening (blown tyre, broken half-shaft, seized engine, locked brakes, collision?); fear, waking in a strange white bed in a strange white room, and nothing moving but your eyeballs—and, maybe, nothing ever *going* to move but your eyeballs.

It can happen to any of us, of course, and to hundreds of us it does, every day, every night, year in and year out, though usually we are spared wondering if it will happen; and we should *all* be kind and, if we thought about it, we would be; a racing-driver does think about it. Not all, not all, granted. Some never think about it, or almost never, or only once, and then put it aside. These are unimaginative men, or they are careful men, expert, intelligent planners, men who know their limits and will stay well and truly inside the boundaries of them, not most of the time but *all* the time. Men like Tazio Nuvolari and Stirling Moss are temperamentally unsuited to this kind of thinking. When they got into the motor-car they intended to go in harm's way; they intended to go all the way up to the boundary line, and, if need be, as they both did at the Nurburg Ring a quarter of a century apart, well over it. Men like this may say, as Nuvolari did when someone asked him if he was not afraid:

"Tell me, do you think you will die in bed? You do? Then, where do you find the courage to get into it every night?"

Or, they may say, as Moss does: "I never think of danger. It never occurs to me that I may be hurt. If it did, I wouldn't

get into the car. I'm not that brave." What Nuvolari and
Moss meant, each of us must decide for himself. One thing
is certain: since each of them spoke with terrible crashes
and desperate injuries behind him, the things they said cannot be as simple as they seem.

They were much alike, Nuvolari and Moss, aside from
being perhaps the two best, in the profession they shared,
among all the men who've attempted it. Like Moss, Nuvolari
had a great head for detail, nothing forgotten, a place for
everything and everything in its place; he had a quick temper
under careful control; he was taut, strong, over-energized,
and a kind man. Women who have known Stirling Moss
remark his force, his impact, and his kindness, which they
usually cite as thoughtfulness; those of them who know they
are listed in a series of little black books, with coded identi-
fiers and reminders, are not much the less moved. Oddly,
although he may complain that the day is a ruin if he comes
into London airport at midnight and doesn't have a date
waiting, Moss is psychologically out of phase with the Don
Juan role. Fidelity to one woman would be his choice, but
he has romantic and unrealistic standards to which he wants
that woman to conform, and so he is always searching. He
may find her. Men have done it. Men have made twenty-
eight straight passes at the dice table, too. But not many
men. In any case, the girls in the Mini were not candidates.
We turned off and left them behind.

We went into the ground-floor flat in Earls Court Road.
I unlimbered a tape-recorder, Stirling put a plug on it, connected it and tested it carefully. There was an electric fire
in the grate. It was a cold day; a heavy, wet wind leaned on
the side of the building.

Unlike some drivers, Moss doesn't like to talk about cars,
and he doesn't like to fiddle about with them, either. Ob-

viously, cars bore him. "The motor-car is my business,"
he says. "It's not a pleasure." He is like a painter asked
about brushes. He's interested in what a man can do with a
car, and what they can do with him. He is little intrigued
by the device itself.

"It's odd, how many commonly-held ideas are all wrong,"
he said. "The notion that you need a lot of raw courage to
race, for instance. Actually I don't think courage is any
advantage at all except in certain special circumstances. It's
a disadvantage. If a driver has too much courage it's difficult for him to discover his limitations until perhaps it's too
late. We've both known people who had more courage than
judgement and they are no longer with us. Or you see
people who go in over their heads too early and *they're* not
with us any more. Or you see others do it, like John Surtees,
but he has so much sensitivity and ability and sheer *feeling*
for a vehicle that he should get away with it; you have a
conviction that even if he loses it he'll get the thing straight
before he hits what he's going to hit and he'll hit it with
the right end of the car and all that. And others you just
know that if they can hit in the wrong way they'll bloody-
well hit in the wrong way and the wrong place. You see
drivers who have tremendous accidents and sometimes
they're not as bad drivers as you think; and others like poor
Pete Collins [killed at the Nurburg Ring in 1958] have a
slight one and he's not with us any more—and Pete didn't
really drive over his head.

"Enzo Ferrari told me that he believes that the accidents
happen before the man gets into the car. In many cases I'm
inclined to agree with him. Attitude of mind and mental
condition and *knowing* when you're dropping off in effec-
tiveness . . . physical fatigue comes on slowly, slowly, it
could be measured with a micrometer; you're giving energy

gradually but continually, and then quite suddenly you're into your reserve, you're a fifth-second slow in reacting to something, and perhaps that's when you leave us. . . .

"I don't know what makes me go on. People often ask me, do you think of giving up racing when someone's killed, a close friend perhaps? Yes, surely. You must think, there but for the grace of God . . . but you hope of course that you have a little more experience or a little more ability or a little more luck or a little more something, and so it's not going to happen to you. If I were killed racing I wouldn't want any driver to give up racing or even pull out of the race it happened in . . . it's not going to do me any good. [Talking to Walter Cronkite of the Columbia Broadcasting System in the United States, Moss said: "I never say to anybody: 'See you next week.' If they say it, I say: 'Well, I hope so.'"] I understand racing, I know it may happen, and if I knew any way to lessen the chance I would do it—as I think I do now. I race as safely as I know how— with the possible exception that I drive cars that are more likely to fail than others, they are less robust, and in that I'm foolish, and I know it. But other factors enter there— my wish to drive British non-factory cars, and so on. . . .

"But there's no point iñ looking into the past. I won't do it. I will not allow myself to live in the past, not the slightest bit. The only way I know what I did yesterday is to look it up in my diary. I keep a full diary, and I do it every night no matter what. If I'm conscious, I make an entry in my diary. If someone's in bed with me, I just say: 'Excuse me, sweetie, whilst I write a couple of thing in m'book.' And do you know, sometimes I find it difficult to remember, at night, what I've done that day, never mind yesterday? I upset my friends. I said to David Haynes: 'You must see this terrific film,' and he said: 'Look, we saw it together last Thursday.' I said to him: 'My God next year you must come with me to South Africa' and he said: 'You know, I was the one with you in Africa' . . . he understands, it's just that there's so much going on today and tomorrow and next week, and I *must* think that way, because there are so many heartbreaks for me in racing that if I worried about yesterday . . . as it is now, I can lose a race, I can lose the world championship on Sunday and I can be out enjoying myself on Monday, and I *mean* enjoying myself. Nothing is sillier than this notion that drivers have a death-wish. Most of them enjoy life infinitely more than the average man, and it's nothing to do with eat, drink and be merry for tomorrow we die, either. [Oddly, the Marquis de Portago said the same thing to me, in almost precisely the same words.] I've been accused of living a 29-hour day and I plead guilty, with pleasure. I live for the day.

"You could say it's an odd life, Ken, and I'd agree, but it's like a story I remember your telling me in a letter a long time ago, about the man who was told the roulette game was crooked, and he said: 'Yes, I know—but it's the only game in town.'

"In the end, one has one's work—the only game in town. I wouldn't want any other work. Obviously the major satisfaction in my life is racing, and I enjoy it even when I'm frustrated, sometimes I think maybe *most* when I'm frustrated; I think, I can't damned well win, I've lost five laps in the pit, it's impossible to win now, mathematically impossible, but then I begin to think, well, my God, even if I can't win I'm going to damned well go, and then I can enjoy really fast motoring, for the exhilaration of it and because I'm trying to prove something to myself; they may have five laps on me, but I'm going to take one back, and the lap record is always there to be broken. . . . [Here

Stirling is, eerily, describing precisely the situation he was to be in four days later at Goodwood.]

"Another thing, you know, you say to yourself, let's really get going, let's try to drive the perfect lap, all the way around and not one mistake, not one mile an hour slow or ten revs down, and this to me is an interesting thing. Often I turn to myself and say, well, let's try to turn one perfect lap. Invariably something somewhere isn't just quite right, and you say, well, that's finished, now let's try another, try again. I've never made a perfect lap, although people have said I have.

"You go through a corner absolutely flat out, right on the ragged edge, but absolutely in control, on your own line to an inch, the car just hanging there, the tyres as good as geared to the road, locked to it, and yet you know that if you ask one more mile an hour of the car, if you put another five pounds of side-thrust on it, you'll lose the whole flaming vehicle as surely as if someone had smeared the road with six inches of grease; so you stay just this side of that fraction of extra speed, that fraction of extra weight that could ruin everything, and perhaps kill you to boot, you're on top of it all, and the exhilaration, the thrill is tremendous, you say to yourself, all right, you bastards, top that one, match it, even, and you feel like a painter who has just put the last brush-stroke on a canvas, after years of trying to catch a certain expression—it's rewarding. And you must grant that it's not monotonous. No art can be monotonous, and I believe that driving, as practised by some very few people in the world, is an art-form, and is related to ballet. I believe that when someone like Alfred Neubauer uses the term 'artist' in relation to a driver, he knows what he's talking about. Driving is certainly like ballet in that it is all discipline, rhythm, movement. I've had people tell me it's a mad thing to say that driving can be an art. After all, we can all of us drive, can't we? Of course, and we can all sing, and write, and most of us can dance, and draw some kind of picture, but some do it a little better than others, that's all.

"I don't say that driving is an art-form *wholly* comparable with ballet. Certainly it's not creative in the sense that choreography is creative or that the composition of music for ballet is creative, but I think that in *execution* it is comparable. Ballet is movement, isn't it, rhythmic and disciplined movement, gracefully performed . . . the man doesn't do it, the driver, he makes the car do it . . . of course, to see it you must be at the right corner at the right moment. The straights don't count, the straights are just there to join the corners. But in the corners there is something to see, sometimes."

"The straight is the place to listen," I said to Stirling. "A few weeks ago I was listening to a race in France on the radio, and cars were going past the microphone, and I said to somebody who was with me: 'That Ferrari is in F-sharp' —and of course I was told it was an absurd idea, I was out of my mind. And a couple of weeks later Anthony Hopkins, the composer, you know who he is, was on B.B.C., and he was talking about the musical sound cars make passing a given point. They're all quite different. Of course they have to be wound right out, the faster the engine's turning, the better; and there's that up and down as they come and go past a point, you know, the Doppler Effect. Of course you hear none of it, driving."

"No . . . but I've sat out a few races, don't forget!"

"I have an idea for a ballet, the central theme, a thesis: 'I don't know where I'm going, but I will be there ahead of you.'"

Stirling said: "At first, that sounds funny, but there's nothing funny about it, nothing at all."

"No, there isn't."

"In any case," Stirling said, "driving is a dance, in a way. And it's like ski-ing, too, very much like ski-ing . . . the same, but never the same, never monotonous . . . monotony in life would drive me mad. I can't bear inactivity; I get disheartened sometimes when I stop moving. If you turned to me right now and said: 'We've finished, you're to go home and sit down and think for a while', I wouldn't dream of doing it. I would find that very bad. I fill every moment. When you leave me here Ken Gregory and some people are coming for a meeting. After that I'm going out to dinner. Then I'm going dancing. [Moss has been known to dance from early evening until dawn, almost without stopping.] I don't know how long I'll stay out, but one thing I'm sure of, when I go to bed tonight I hope to be very tired, because I don't want to think, I don't *like* thinking, unless it's about a specific solvable problem. As far as life is concerned, and what life is going to offer me, I find it terribly depressing. When I look at the future I find it terribly depressing!"

He spoke so vehemently, and it was so unlike anything I had heard him say before, that I was surprised. "Do you really, Stirling?" I said.

"Yes, terribly, because I can't see, in the ultimate, what there can be of happiness. I know that to some people achievement in business, in work, is happiness. To me it's not, it's a fulfilment, but not happiness, or not necessarily happiness. It's a pleasure, but pleasure isn't happiness. My idea of happiness seems Utopian to me and it may seem absurd to you, so absurd I'm surprised I can bring myself to tell you, but it is to be married, and have two or three children, and a house in the country, if you like, and to go away for two weeks on holiday—and most of all, most importantly, to be able to *accept* that life as happiness. Do you understand? To be able to *accept* it, that's the whole heart of the matter. I'm trying to describe an attitude, I think, more than a way of life. A matter of *balance*. I know what it is, but I can't accept it, not at the moment. I'm hoping that with maturity I will be able to, or that at least some form of compromise with it will be possible. I'm not unhappy. I've had some tremendously good times. But right now I'm in a state of suspended animation, in a transition period which is tolerable, and which keeps me from being depressed. . . . I dance, I run about, I do a bit of designing and this and that, it's activity, I keep my finger in the dike, it's not going to patch the bloody thing but at least it's stopping the water pouring in. I'm waiting for maturity to come to me, and I'm doing what I can to bring it. I don't know if one ever feels happiness, or if contentment is the maximum we can hope for. As I said, I'm not unhappy. If I were to be killed tomorrow I wouldn't feel that thirty-two of my thirty-two years had been unhappy. . . ."

We talked, and the thin brown tape, shuffling through the recorder-heads, silently took it down. Dusk sifted out of a wet London sky. We had given ourselves three hours, and at five minutes short of seven the tape ran out. He made me a drink. He couldn't find a bottle-opener for the orange squash he wanted and I fiddled the top off with my knife. We talked about some other people for a few minutes. He telephoned for a taxi. I told the driver to go to Charing Cross. As I opened the cab door I looked back. Moss was standing in the middle of the little room, looking through the window. I waved to him. He waved, and moved away across the room. He looked grim and, somehow, weirdly, sheathed all in grey, or white. I was suddenly and inexplicably immersed in a crushing sadness and in pity for him. The cab moved away. I felt frightened, and very nearly ill. I remembered the only time such a thing had happened to me before, ten years ago, on a hot July day in Connecticut, again for no reason—except that at that moment, 1500 miles away, as I was to know later, a doctor was saying of my son: "He may live forty-eight hours, but I doubt it."

By next morning I had put all that out of my mind. I was in Belgium on Easter Monday and I didn't see Stirling Moss again until early June, when I went to the Atkinson Morley Hospital. I stayed a couple of hours. Judy Carne did a scalding imitation of her Hollywood manicurist phoning a boy-friend. I told the old story about Beatrice Lillie, Lady Peel, and the butcher's wife. The tape-recorder man came, tacking shyly into the room against a gale of laughter. I left.

"Come back soon," Stirling said. "I'm not going to hang about here forever."

CHAPTER III

"Ride on! Rough-shod if need be, smooth-shod
if that will do, but ride on!"
Charles Dickens

CHAPTER III

THE extraordinary concern and affection the British people show for Stirling Moss cannot be explained by his eminence as a sports figure.* The British people have known many great sportsmen, and they have usually viewed them with comparative calm and equanimity, but during the decade 1952–62, let us say, Stirling Moss has been one of the most prominent figures in the United Kingdom. Other formidable accomplishers, sportsmen, athletes, film stars, scientists, politicians, have stopped upon the stage, stayed a bit, and slipped away. But still today, and this is written nearly a full year after Goodwood, when Stirling Moss comes down a jet-ramp at London Airport, it's news. Why?

I thought I knew, but I asked a more knowledgeable man, a Fleet Street editor who has seen Page One celebrities come and go for twenty-odd years.

"It's because he was a knight in armour," the editor said, "rushing out of the castle to do battle in foreign lands, and coming back, sometimes with the prize and sometimes without it; sometimes bloody on his shield and sometimes not—but always in a hurry to go back and have another bash at the heathen."

Exactly.

It is a cliché to say that people in the mass sense sincerity, and sense true purpose, but they do. It can be demonstrated

* My London housekeeper, who had never seen a motor-race, and had never seen Moss excepting on television, asked me to tell him to please shave off his beard, she didn't like it. Then she added: "He is very dear to us."

85

under rigid laboratory conditions that mass judgement is more nearly accurate than individual judgement: if people are asked to estimate the weight of an object by sight and touch, the trend toward the correct answer will rise precisely in proportion to the size of the group. The British people in the mass have known that Stirling Moss has driven to make money, and for personal renown, but they have sensed that he drove to show the flag as well. I think that if he had been born very wealthy, indifferent to the necessity of earning a living, and able to build or buy any car, he would have done the same thing with his life that he has done. I think he has wanted above all to show the world a Briton winning. He has been fervently patriotic, in big as well as in little ways: Alf Francis has told, in his book *Racing Mechanic,* how Moss, when he first drove a Maserati, wouldn't even take the car out on the circuit, in its Italian racing red, until two Union Jack transfers had been put on it.

So have other men in racing done this. Dick Seaman did it in the 1930's. Like Moss, he drove for Mercedes-Benz, and he was the first Englishman ever to win the German *Grand Prix* (he won it in a good year, too, 1938, and put Hitler into a fury). But Seaman's career, unhappily, was short. What of Raymond Mays and Peter Berthon and the whole B.R.M. staff, stoically soaking up a decade and more of hard work and bitter disappointment? And Jack Brabham and Graham Hill won the championship of the world, and in British cars, something that Moss never did.

It is in no way disparaging the British drivers now dominating the world's *grand prix* circuits, Graham Hill, Jimmy Clark, John Surtees, to say that any one of them could be champion of the world three years running and not know the determined affection the British people shower on Moss, who was never champion and never will be.

An actor who is a devotee of motor-racing said to me: "When a man has that weird and elusive star-quality, whatever it is, the thing that makes other men want to stand him a drink, and women want to take him in their arms, whether to mother him or make love to him, then his actual success-failure ratio doesn't matter. Did you notice Orson Welles pointing out the other day that Greta Garbo, the greatest film star of all time, never had a film that made much money? What about the way the Americans have idolized Jack Dempsey for nearly four decades? After all, Gene Tunney beat Dempsey, not once but twice—but Dempsey will still stop traffic in the same street where Tunney will go unnoticed. Moss never *needed* to win the championship of the world, strangely enough."

The Dempsey-Tunney parallel is apt. Tunney, 'Gentleman Gene', amateur Shakespearian scholar, friend of George Bernard Shaw, came to the ring with calm and measured tread, in the pink of condition, his battle thought out as much as a battle can be, prepared to extend himself if he had to, but carefully, intelligently. Tunney fought as a sensible thinking man ought to fight, won the heavyweight championship of the world, made millions out of it, retired undefeated to a gracious and secure private life.

Dempsey came into the arena almost running towards the ring, black-jowled, jumpy, scowling. Watching him, one felt that if the referee came over and said: "Jack, the other fellow wants to fight with these double-bitted woodsman's axes instead of gloves," Dempsey would have said: "Right. Give me one of 'em and get the hell out of the way!"

Watching Stirling Moss 'rush out of the castle' as the Fleet Street man put it, the public have had the same feeling about him. They thought of him as going alone into France and Sweden and Denmark and Portugal and Spain and Germany, Italy, South Africa, Morocco, Monaco, Switzerland, the United States, Canada, Ireland, Argentina, Cuba, Mexico, Australia, New Zealand, Belgium and wherever not, for one purpose: to fight. They felt that the reputation of Great Britain was safe with him, before the world. They were certain he'd win more times than he'd lose, and that in any case, win or lose, 99 times in 100 he'd finish on his feet. I suspect that Moss's fantastic comeback after the 1960 accident at Spa excited the pride of Britons as not many things had since the war. When a Belgian doctor told him that he would have to spend six months in plaster up to his neck, Moss said: "Put me on an aeroplane and ship me to London." Russell Brockbank's cartoon in *Punch* told a great deal. Moss was trying to get out of that hospital as some men try to dig their way out of prison. I remember telephoning him from New York about three weeks after the accident.

"How are you really?" I said. "I hear all kinds of things."

"I'm in good shape," he said. "I'm going bike-riding tomorrow."

"You mean on a stationary bike?"

"No, I mean a real bike."

"You're out of your mind. What happens if you fall off the thing?"

"I don't intend to fall off."

Reading over the last few hundred words, a friend said to me: "I think Stirling is more Tunney than Dempsey—thinking, a planner, always in condition, always ready."

I said: "No. Dempsey was usually in condition, too. *But even if he wasn't,* he was ready. He'd go, condition or

88

"*I see young Stirling's broken out.*"

Reproduced by permission of Punch.

no condition. He kept nothing back, and that's why his name is magic. You could beat Dempsey, but you couldn't make a loser out of him, and you can't make a loser out of Moss. Tunney had Dempsey flat on the deck, but half the people who saw the fight refused to believe it."

Stirling Moss's personality is complicated, and he is competent at guarding it. The man is not simple; the way to the centre of him makes Hampton Court Maze look as open and straight as The Mall. I don't claim to have been there, in the years I've known him, but I do know that under the urbanity, under the good humour and *politesse,* under the flat, bland, masked face that I have watched as he walked silently away from dry petrol tanks, flat batteries and flawed gear boxes ("Few people can hide their real feelings the way he can," Alf Francis said), he carries the one thing that distinguishes all the great competitors from the also-rans, the spear-carriers: the thing the fight people call killer-instinct. Moss wouldn't rather be dead than a loser, he doesn't want to die to win—but he'll take the chance. A man who is a spear-carrier at heart can be a famous competitor, husbanding himself, watching his chances, thinking of the future, of his career as a rounded whole, and he can go a long, long way. But the real competitor can only try that line, half-heartedly and briefly, before the thing that has made him takes over, before, as drivers say, the power comes in, and his foot goes down. ("One's a race-driver, or one's not.") It is not a matter of another few thousand pounds, or another silver cup, the laurel wreath, a kiss from a pretty girl, more starting-money next time, a better contract from the tyre-company next year, none of that nonsense, none of that mere careerist bilge, it is nothing that can be shared with a living soul, indeed many of the bitter-end competitors, the killers, hold it so secret they'll deny they have it, it is a private thing,

the dark, driving urge man has known since he came creep-
ing out of the cave, the wish for identity, the grinding need
to lift one's face out of the sea of the faces of the mob, to
mark oneself and what one stands for, because that is worth
while, that is immortality, and the price to be paid for it is
only a transient thing. Some prime ministers and presidents
have known this, but not all. Some stone-masons have
known it, but not all, and some racing-drivers, but not
all.

Juan Manuel Fangio had so much power, so much skill,
so much intelligence, so much of everything that some
people, hearing him speak, in a tired, whispery monotone,
watching him drive, smooth as oil on glass, wholly un-
dramatic nearly all of the time, would say: "Old Chueco
is so good, he doesn't need to care, he doesn't have to fight"
—forgetting the years when he drove home-made Ford and
Chevrolet specials in the ferocious Trans-Andean road-races
of South America, some of them 6,000 miles long. Then, in
1956 at Monaco, Moss started to run away from him, and
amazed crowds saw the most skilful car-conserver since
Caracciola spin his Ferrari, knocking two other cars out of
the race, and then bounce it off a kerb, buckling a wheel.
He left that one and took Peter Collins's car, but still couldn't
catch Moss, though he broke the course record trying. At
the Nurburg Ring in 1957, challenged by Mike Hawthorn
and Peter Collins, he rounded on them like a baited bear,
and in the process of giving both of them a thorough beating,
broke the lap record ten times.

Fangio was Moss's model, his teacher in the more esoteric,
advanced techniques of driving, but he had nothing to teach
him in *sang-froid,* in covering over, with civility and
urbanity, the bone-deep will to win. ("We are all friends,"
Moss said one day, speaking of the other drivers, "but once

the race starts, no one expects to hear anyone say: 'After you, m'lord.'" I was reminded of Wilbur Shaw, a gentleman, who might give another driver the shirt off his back before a race and buy him a drink afterwards, but during it would run the man into a concrete wall at 140 miles an hour if he wouldn't move over.)

"At Bari, in 1950," Stirling told me, "soon after I'd joined H.W.M., I was leading from Fangio for a bit, and Farina, although a lap behind. They were both in Alfas, I had a Formula II H.W.M. Fangio was third, Farina was just behind me, and I think he was annoyed, after all I was a new boy and he was a very important figure. In any case, he came alongside me going into a corner and just stayed there, he shut the gate on me, as the Americans say. He gave me the alternative of slowing down or going into a wall. But I slowed right down, I got round his tail, and then, because what he'd done had put him on the wrong line, I went through just ahead of him. I looked back and Fangio, just behind us, was laughing his head off."

The roughest thing Moss remembers doing on a circuit? —"At Roskilde one time there was a chap in a Ferrari, a Swede, who would *not* let me past. I took it for two or three laps, even people in the crowd were shaking their fists at him. Finally, just before a slow corner, the front of my car touched his tail and spun him. He went on—but I had got past him!"

Stirling once told me that when he had lost a race, he could put it out of his mind and sleep like a baby, but that the night after he'd won was likely to be sleepless. This is the competitor's typical reaction. For the ordinary man, the situation would be exactly reversed. Losing, he would be full of fury and frustration, no more able to sleep than to fly by flapping his arms. I have seen men in this case stay wide-awake under a dose of Seconal that would stun a Shetland pony. But, winning, they feel fulfilled, content, and they sleep in peace. The real competitor looks at losing, loathing it, shoves it savagely out of his mind and goes to sleep. He must, or he'll unhinge himself. It is winning that keeps *him* awake, because it means so much to him, it is fulfilment, his *raison d'être,* and though he conceal it under however much urbanity and ritual sportsmanship, it shakes him through and through, it stirs him to his soul.

Someone said recently, with an air of discovery, that the British people are at their best in war, and have always been, that they *like* fighting, that they like bucking the odds, and that however savagely and bitterly they fight, they are sustained by observance of the proprieties, by maintenance at all cost of an air of calm, civilized good temper.

The two things do not always go together. I think people quietly admire the hard fighter, and they admire the man who shows grace under pressure, even if it is only mild pressure. But they reserve their hearts for the man whom their instincts tell them is a killer, a bitter-ender, *and* a man capable of winning all he wants in the world, or losing everything he owns, in such fashion that one can't tell, watching him, which has happened. This, they feel, is British behaviour.

Stirling Moss is British.

One did not watch Stirling Moss drive for long without noticing that he almost invariably waved as he passed another car. This wave was pleasant to see, a kind of salute, given with the hand held vertically, graceful without excessive movement, imperious as well as polite.

I was standing at the bottom of the pit straight at Sebring one hot morning, a place where one can almost look into the cars. A photographer was with me. Stirling, coming out of the U-turn faster than most, as was his wont, ate up a Porsche as he went by us, giving the man his patented wave.

"Have you ever noticed," the photographer said, "that Moss always thanks another driver for letting him pass?"

I laughed. "Yes," I said, "I've noticed that. Of course in this case he was thanking the man for nothing, wasn't he, because the only way C—— could have prevented Mossie's passing would have been to shoot him."

"Oh, I don't know," the photographer said. "He didn't have to move over."

"The rules say he did," I said. "They'd have hit him with a blue flag half-way down the straight if he hadn't. Anyway, it's wide here, Moss would have run around him."

"I still think it's a pleasant gesture," my friend said. "It shows the camaraderie that exists among really big-league drivers, and I like to see him do it."

"Camaraderie, my foot," I said. "If that pig he's driving holds together all day, you'll get to see him wave to everybody out there, and I daresay you'll like it better than they will, too."

"Why?"

"Because he's mostly thanking them for nothing, and that's not all he's doing."

"You fascinate me," my friend said. "Tell me, what else is he doing?"

"He's waving goodbye to them," I said.

No stronger competitive instinct than Moss's has ever appeared in sports, I am convinced, and I have outraged a lot of people by saying so. That motoring enthusiasts can be annoyed by the picture of Stirling Moss as a brutal competitor is illustrative of the fantastic discipline the man has imposed on himself, and of the skill with which he has originated and erected his public character.

"Watching Stirling Moss before a race," a man said to me about five years ago, "the absolute picture of calm, is to understand real sportsmanship. For him, the game is everything, *form* is everything, and winning or losing is of not the slightest importance."

I won't quote my reply. It was both rude and profane.

That Stirling Moss was usually calm before a race is true. This is rare. Juan Belmonte used to say: "If we had to sign the contracts an hour before the *corrida* there would be no one in the ring when the bulls come out."

I had a conversation with a well-known driver just before a race, and when I took it up again that night I discovered that he not only didn't recall what we'd talked about, he couldn't remember our speaking at all! Nothing of that sort ever happened to Moss. I remember almost bumping into him just off a starting-grid one day, before I knew him well, and I smiled and kept on, having learned from the experience I mentioned above that it was best not to talk to drivers just before the off. But Moss had something he wanted to tell me; he took my arm and walked along with me for three or four minutes.

Then he said: "Excuse me, Ken, I must find m'hat," and went off for his helmet. Five minutes later, he was motoring.

"I don't mind anyone talking to me before a start," he has said to me. "I don't care in the least. If I'm sitting in the car, a boy can ask me for an autograph. I'm happy to talk about anything, a play I saw the night before, a girl, up to the moment I start the engine, I couldn't care less. I've done my practice, I reckon to know the course, I reckon the car to be ready, I can't make a plan, I can't foresee what's to happen when fifteen of us pile into the first corner, so why should I bother thinking about it? Time enough for that when we get there. I was giving a chap a radio interview one day, in the States, sitting on the starting-grid; we were chatting away, and suddenly I realized the race was going to start in sixty seconds. I had almost forgotten about it!"

It would be interesting to be able to look into Moss's head as he switches off his urbane, gay, smiling self, to switch on Moss the competitor and the engine at the same time. (I know a veteran airlines captain who does the same thing, in a slightly different fashion. Sitting in the front end of a trans-Atlantic jet, waiting, perhaps, for a delayed load of passengers, he's amusing, witty, relaxed, he and his crew are just old friends killing time together. With him the change-over comes when he draws on a pair of pigskin gloves, without which, I think, he couldn't fly. When the gloves go on, the temperature in the cockpit drops about ten degrees, and thereafter anyone who speaks to him had best have a "Captain" or a "sir" on the end of the sentence, as well as a good reason for speaking at all.)

The reason the competitive attitude so intrigues us is that it's a distillate of life. And the occasional appearance of a really strong competitive instinct in one of the four elemental games—fighting, mountain-climbing, the *corrida,* and motor-racing—is more compelling, naturally, than its appearance in, say, swimming or pole-vaulting or one of the stick-and-ball games. Knowing how the great mountaineer Albert Frederick Mummery of Dover went up the Chamonix Aiguilles or how Edward Whymper did the Matterhorn or how Stirling Moss ran the Mille Miglia, we know something of how life may be lived, and perhaps should be lived, and we have seen this thing in minutes instead of years.

This is not to denigrate the great spirits who appear in the lesser games. The American baseball player Harold 'Pete' Reiser, held by many to have been the most competitive player of modern times, was carried off the field incapacitated or unconscious eleven times in fourteen years of play: five times because, running to get under a high ball, he had refused to take his eyes off it, lest he lose it in the sun or the field-lights, and went full tilt into the concrete wall that borders the outer perimeters of most major-league baseball parks.

It is a peculiarity of the real competitor that he is indifferent to being hurt. The intellectual, the spiritual aspect of elemental competition against other men has become so weighty that it transcends consideration of the corporal, he no longer cares about being hurt excepting that injury keeps him out of the game. (Left to himself, he will invariably go back before he's fit.) A peculiarity of the real competitor who has a major talent—the two things do not necessarily go together—is that he likes to handicap himself, to make the game harder. Thus Mummery would not use pitons, he thought them base, a thing for cheaters, although many mountaineers will hardly go up a flight of stairs without a sackful of pitons and a hammer to drive them. Moss's addiction to non-factory cars is illustrative.

The real competitor, if he lives long enough, comes inevitably to the realization that the ultimate victory is the victory over self: when the years of self-discipline and self-denial are past, the years of study and training and practice to exhaustion are over, the man understands, suddenly or slowly as the case may be, that the being *able* to win is what matters; that the formal victory itself, the laurel wreath, is then only a statistic, a thing of no consequence, and he no longer even wants it.

The real competitor sees no limitations. He wants to beat the whole world. If he's a simple man, like John L. Sullivan, the legendary heavyweight fighter, he'll say so. Sullivan used to announce from the ring: "In a fair fight, I will whip any man born of woman. Yours truly, John L. Sullivan." He handicapped himself with brandy. In the course of a long fight, Sullivan would empty a bottle of cognac. He was much admired. In 1887 a crowd, trying to get near him, broke up the carriage in which he was riding down the Haymarket.

A complex personality behaves with more civility, although he may wish to beat every other man in the world, and at everything. (Wilbur Shaw was so bothered by the fact that other men could drive railway engines, whilst he could not, that he badgered a railway company into teaching him).

Dominating one of the most competitive endeavours man knows, for more than a decade, entering more races than anyone else had ever done, and winning more of them, was not enough for Stirling Moss. He started so many ancillary activities that they would occupy most people through an eight-hour day. He is no threat to J. Paul Getty as a business-man, but if one enterprise fails he is always ready to start another. He has the obsessive concern with details that so often marks the man who can't find *enough* to do. I am almost surprised that Stirling doesn't type his own letters. (Come to think of it, I have a number of letters from him that he did type—at least some amateur did them!)

The real competitor is not easy to live with, when he is on the way up, and when he is at the top, because he is driven to compete with everybody, he wants to do everything better, he wants to dominate everyone around him, his friends, his associates, his employees, his wife. This is the deepest need in his nature and allowance must be made for it. It has made him what he is; without it we would never have heard of him.

CHAPTER IV

"... the men who drove them ... pursuing a
private vision of life few of us can understand."
Robert Daley

DRAMATIC critics think that they are best qualified to decide who's a good actor, and who is better and who is best, and the book critics do the same with writers, and the motoring journalists like to make rankings among drivers. This is all very well, and professional critics —the word really means 'judges' after all—do nearly always form sound opinions. But no critic can gauge the true ability of an actor with the force and precision of another actor who has stood beside the man during 102 performances of *King Lear*. The same thing is true in other professions; most emphatically I think it is true of driving. The man sitting in the press-box, at race after race, sees a good deal, but he doesn't see what a driver sees, running beside someone else for hundreds of miles.

"Of the drivers I've watched," Stirling Moss says, "I put Fangio on top, insofar as the top branch of racing is concerned: Formula One, *grand prix*. He was not at ease in sports car events. For example, he very much disliked the *Mille Miglia* and would not run in it unless he had to. But, characteristically, when he went, he went all the way. You remember 1953, when a track-rod broke on his Alfa-Romeo and he still came in second, steering with one wheel, the other flopping loose. You want to try that sometime, boy. I would recommend you to try it on an airport, though, and slowly, not on a two-lane road, flat-out. Fangio didn't run in rallies, he didn't do land-speed records or hill-climbs or anything of that sort—but don't forget that for thirteen years in South America, from 1936 to 1949, he ran in some of the hairiest races you could imagine, and won a lot of them, too, in cars a sensible man would hesitate to sit in.

"Fangio could get into an absolute bastard of a car and draw the maximum out of it; or get into a beautiful car and take everything there was in it. And I don't care how fast you went or anybody went, boy, he could *always* go quicker; and give him a dog and he'd still go quicker. [Innes Ireland has said of Moss: "You may think you know your own car and are getting the most out of it, but Moss will step into it cold and go faster."] That's in *grand prix* cars, of course; in sports cars I always felt that I could beat him.

"But in *grand prix* cars he was fantastic. His record speaks for itself. He won twenty-five races of the first importance. No one who ever sat in a racing-car made fewer mistakes than Fangio. No one. The man's judgement was just incredibly good, never mind his sheer ability, his strength, his quickness and all the rest of it. The only time he was badly hurt, the only real accident he had in G.P. racing, when he broke his neck at Monza in 1952 in a Maserati, it was due to bad judgement, yes, but *before* the race, not during it. Instead of making his own arrangements, and being sure about it, Fangio had accepted an invitation to fly to Monza from Ireland with another driver, and the fellow forgot about it and went off without him; Fangio flew to Paris, found the weather bad, and had to rent a car and drive like mad over the mountains. Naturally enough when he got to Monza he wasn't really fit to drive in a race and he had this incident. But that was the only time he ever hurt himself, as far as I know.

"The best classroom of all time, I'm convinced, was the

spot about two car-lengths behind Juan Manuel Fangio. I learned more there than I ever did anywhere else.

"I never saw Tazio Nuvolari. I know Enzo Ferrari rates Nuvolari and me over Fangio. But for me, he must remain the best."

"Stirling, let me interrupt you here," I said. "Tell me: did Fangio let you win the British Grand Prix in 1955. Did he give you that one?"

"Ken, I honestly don't know. I can tell you that there was no pre-arrangement. Neubauer didn't run the team that way. Fangio might have done. I was running first, he was just behind me. I passed someone and I thought, right, here's my chance, and I drove like a maniac and opened up ground on him. Going into the last corner, I was still ahead and coming out I knew he couldn't make it. I pulled well over, I waved to him to come through . . . but I knew he hadn't a chance without another 40 horsepower. Our cars were as nearly identical as Mercedes could build them and he just hadn't the power to catch me.

"So, I don't know, and I never shall, I suppose, because certainly I wouldn't ask Fangio. The truth, as nearly as I can come to it, is that he could not have caught me at the end, but that he *might* have let me grab those few yards of lead earlier on. If he did do it, it was very skilful, very subtle —but with Fangio, of course, it would be. He did everything that way. That's why there's almost no one who can be compared with him.

"Certainly Alberto Ascari was wonderfully good. Farina and Villoresi never impressed me very much, but they were well along in their careers when I came up; perhaps the fire was going out for them. As you know, I copied Farina's posture, his attitude at the wheel. You'll hear it said I did this because I knew the straight-arm position was efficient.

Nonsense. I didn't know anything of the kind. I took it over because I liked the way it looked. One looked better, driving that way. I didn't *like* it at all. It felt strange, awkward. But I kept on until in the end I got to the stage where I honestly did like it. And once you get used to it you discover that it is really better to sit well back from the wheel, your arms straight, better for many reasons. Once you know, then it's a strain to go back to the old bent-elbow position. You feel the shortcomings of that attitude. But I didn't know that for a long time.

"Piero Taruffi was an example of a particularly intelligent man in motor-racing. He was never in the very first rank, but he certainly did do a great deal of motor-racing. Most people watching motor-racing don't appreciate Taruffi's kind of intelligence. If a bloke goes into a corner five miles an hour too fast and manages to get around somehow, all crossed up, but still gets around, he's not brave, he's stupid. Taruffi was a good driver in sports cars, and he knew it, and he knew that on his day he'd do well with a Formula One car, and you could certainly put him into one with confidence that he wouldn't wreck it. He was intelligent, he always knew the circuit to an inch, he knew the machinery —after all, he's an engineer—and he understood what being in condition is worth. I reckon Taruffi must have been one of the strongest men in motor-racing. Do you remember the size of his forearms? Tremendous. I think it's splendid that he finally won the *Mille Miglia*. Imagine, he ran that race thirteen times. It was a great achievement—he ran alone, you know, I'm sure he knew the roads blindfolded— and he deserved to win. I would be unhappy, I would think it farcical, if somebody less intelligent than Taruffi had won the last-ever *Mille Miglia,* just by sticking his foot into it and going in over his head. Although of course if you go into a 1,000-mile open-road race with the idea of putting your foot down and leaving it down you may very well not be with us when it's over.

"Of the drivers who are gone . . . I think first of Mike Hawthorn. Mike was champion of the world, after all. He was a great character. Just his presence did a lot for motor-racing, I think, his being such a character. I liked Mike, although we weren't close friends. You know, Ken, I've never been really close friends with another driver."

"I've wondered about that," I said. "There is something in the business that militates against friendship, closeness. It's hard to think of examples. Hawthorn and Collins were big buddies, remember that 'Mon ami mate' bit they had. Portago and Harry Schell seemed almost inseparable at times. Gonzalez and Marimon and Fangio were close."

"All but two of those people you've mentioned aren't with us now," Stirling said, "so we can't really know. And Gonzalez and Marimon were the *only* drivers who were close to Fangio. I'm certain Fangio avoided friendship with drivers."

"The Roman gladiators would take some trouble to avoid forming friendships with each other, you know," I said, "even those who lasted for years, and lived in the same barracks. But surely that was different; after all they might have to kill each other."

"That's extreme," Stirling said. "I'm sure it doesn't apply. Although of course one doesn't like to *see* one's friends killed, either."

"Something around 180 drivers have been killed since the war ended," I said. "Of those, I would think you knew some very well, some only well enough to say hello to—about fifty men."

"Oh, I should think so. All of fifty, I suppose. It's a great many, isn't it?"

"Yes."

"Of course, Mike was killed on the road, not in a race. I should have been astonished if Mike had been killed in a race. Mike didn't have many incidents on the circuit, when you stop to think about it. But he'd have a go, you know. Mike was a fighter, and that's unusual. There aren't many who have that. Mike was something of an all-rounder; he was reasonably competent in sports cars as well as *grand prix* cars. He looked the part, too, didn't he?

"Mike had a great many off days. But when he was on, he was very, very good indeed.

"His death? I think he might have been driving too fast. I drove with him once, on the road. Frightened me to death. Too fast for me. Because you know it's easy to reckon that your ability will get you out of a situation, without realizing that there may be other people working against you. That's more or less what I think happened to Mike. He was going too fast, the road was slippery, he lost the car—the car he was driving tended to over-steer and the engine had been tuned up—and while he would almost certainly have got the car back had he had room for manœuvre, he didn't; there was a lorry in the way.

"It was a most unhappy thing. Mike had retired with the championship. He had a number of business deals in the wind, and probably would have done well. It was a great pity.

"Of men driving today, one thinks of Graham Hill first, naturally, he's the champion of the world. Graham is in my view the ultimate mechanic-driver. Perhaps he is the archetype of the driver of the future; precise, smooth, knowing. Graham is just as smooth as he looks. Given the equipment, he'll go really quickly, he'll stay out of trouble and if it's possible, he'll keep the machine out of trouble. But if your car is faster than Graham's, you have a fair chance of beating him. He is not the type to risk blowing up an engine or going off the road to catch you, nine times in ten.

"Jack Brabham is something like that, too, he's a superior mechanic-driver, and, as you know, a former champion of the world. Jack shows little emotion. He seems to approach driving as a job. He is something like a painter who can produce a Picasso that one can't tell from the original—if he has the original to work from. Jack's a careful driver, and quite smooth for the most part. When he does get roused, you can see it at once: he reverts to the mannerisms of the Australian dirt tracks he grew up on. He starts to move up on the steering wheel, and the tail of the car begins to hang out in the corners. That means that old Jack has decided to get on with it, and the hell with finesse. If there's much of the race left he'll often scrub the tyres. He'll have a go. You remember when he first came up, there was a gag: 'Here comes Jack Brabham round the bend' and the answer was: 'Oh? Which end of the car is first this time?' He's building a car of his own now, as you know, and I can't think of many things that would make me happier than to see him have a really tremendous world-wide success with it.

"The finest race I've seen Jack do was possibly Warwick Farm in Australia this year, '63. He really drove to win. I was glad to see it. Jack's a generous, good-hearted man. One time in New Zealand I had a half-shaft break, Jack had a spare and he gave it to me. He'd have helped put it on if I'd asked him. He knew I might beat him with it—as it turned out, I did—but that wouldn't make any difference to him.

"Champion of the world before Graham Hill was Phil Hill, the first American to hold the title. Phil is damned good in sports cars, and I should think that now Olivier Gendebien has retired there's no one to contend with Phil Hill as the best sports-car driver, particularly in long-distance events. This is interesting, because Phil is emotionally so taut, so over-wrought much of the time that one would think he'd be exhausted from sheer tension inside two hundred miles. Not at all. He's strong, and he must understand relaxation, because he'll run a thousand miles flat-out and with anybody. It's terrible, the tension that builds up in Phil just before a race, though. You can look over at his car and say: 'My God, Phil, the thing's burning!' and he'll jump nine feet into the air. But when the flag drops he's all right.

"I consider him more than competent in *grand prix* cars, a thorough professional. I think his fidelity to Ferrari, while admirable, if you like—nobody has driven so long for Ferrari, you know, eight years I believe Phil did with him—was harmful to his career. In 1956 I asked him to come along with me on Maseratis. He wouldn't and I still think he should have done. I think this year, 1963, will be crucial for Phil.

"Dan Gurney is going to drive for Jack Brabham this year and that is not the worst idea Jack ever had. I consider Gurney to be, right now, one of the best drivers in the world and one of the fastest. Gurney is competitive. He's a man who'll have a go. He won't say: 'The car isn't much good and I won't bother.' He'll go. A very nice man, too. He looks exactly what he is, one of the few human beings I know who does.

"Bruce McLaren is an intelligent character at the wheel, and thoroughly competent. He's come a long way. He knew he could learn a lot from Brabham, and today he could have a go with Jack in matched cars. The best follower, possibly, in motor-racing today. If you get Bruce on your tail, it doesn't much matter how fast you go, boy, he goes as fast. But if you go into the pits and leave him he'll slow a fraction. Let him tuck in behind you, however, and you've got yourself a problem.

"I don't know enough about Tony Maggs to make fair comment. He's a nice fellow and that's all I know about him.

"Trevor Taylor is a Formula Junior Driver on the way up. He's good, all right, and he's with a talented team.

"Jo Bonnier is I think at a peak level, I don't think he will improve further, and he hasn't started falling off, either. He has a lot of experience and he's a good team-driver. Some people find Jo brusque and cold. It's just that he's not a very outgoing, giving man. He would never mislead you.

"Roy Salvadori has a big volume of experience, reasonable ability and sometimes too much fire. I've seen Roy do some fairly dodgey things now and again. On the whole one must say he's been intelligent about his racing.

"The greatest natural talent driving today is probably Jimmy Clark, and I say 'probably' just for form's sake, because I'm convinced Jimmy *is* the best in the world. He's a *born* driver, and, boy, you know the difference between a born driver and a made driver is the difference between night and day, and more. I was having trouble with Jimmy Clark in 1961. Very well, in matched cars I'd beat him, but by 1961 it was plain that Jimmy Clark was just not the boy to take on if one were driving last year's motor-car."

"I remember your writing that to me, I think it was after South Africa," I said. "I thought at the time it was pretty strong language; you were beating plenty of other people with a year-old motor-car."

"Yes, but he was different," Stirling said. "Jimmy's ability is plain; he doesn't need me to point it up, or anyone else. He'd have been champion of the world this year if a silly bolt hadn't come adrift in his Lotus.

"John Surtees is possibly equal to Jimmy Clark in ability but not in the indefinable quality I call race-winningness. I think four-wheeled experience will sort this out. This coming year, with Ferrari, may put him in a light in which we'll suddenly recognize him as the best driver in the world. Other things equal, I think Surtees would have a better chance than Clark. You know what I think of the Ferrari operation. They go motor-racing in a big way at Modena."

"To go back to Surtees' ability, Stirling," I said, "you remarked earlier his feeling for the vehicle, and he certainly does seem to be welded into it, and running on the identical wave-length and all. Do you suppose that some of this affinity for the machinery derives from his competition history on motor-cycles? It must, no?"

"In John's case, I think so. He was one of the all-time best, you know, he won everything in sight, and his sense of balance in the car, side-to-side and fore-and-aft, must be remarkable. He had to develop a fine sense of tyre-adhesion, too, wet and dry, and you know that heavy braking on a bike is very dicey. It would seem motor-bikes must have helped John a lot, but I wouldn't want to be dogmatic about it; I don't really know; motor-bike experience didn't seem to help Geoff Duke much, and he was another who was at the absolute top of the tree."

"I understand. Still, one often notices that good drivers have put in a lot of time with motor-bikes, aircraft, or horses, so that one wonders if it isn't true that in the far-out reaches of race-driving, out in the thin air around nine-tenths and ten-tenths motoring, superior balance doesn't count very heavily."

"I'm sure it does, Ken. I'm sure that the hundreds of times I put horses over the jumps did a great deal for my sense of balance. Portago used to say the same thing."

"Yes. He flew, too, but he said it bored him, he always felt he was standing still, until he came in to land."

"It hasn't excited me very much, I must say, although I shall probably get back to it. It's something I feel I ought to be able to do."

"Brabham's a good pilot, I understand. Innes Ireland, too."

"Yes, they both fly," Stirling said. "I like Innes, you know, and he is a more than competent driver, although he has on days and off days. He's another Mike Hawthorn, a paler Hawthorn might be the best way to put it. He's not sure of himself, Innes."

"He's certainly a pleasant man, forthright and straightforward."

"Yes, in 1961, when the world championship hung on Monza, and I had a very much out-of-date Lotus, Innes came to me and said: 'Take my car.' His was quicker and faster than mine. I thought that was very good of him."

"You did him a favour one time, too."

"Yes, at Monaco, in 1960, he hadn't qualified, and I reckoned I knew the circuit better than he did, had perhaps a faster line here and there, so I said: 'Right, follow me around,' and he did, and qualified. Innes is another who'll have a go. There may be smoother drivers, but he'll go.

"Fangio was so smooth, it was hard to find anyone to compare with him. After all, Alberto Ascari was rather better than just good, he was very good indeed. He may have been as fast as Fangio; I didn't think he was, but Mike Hawthorn thought so. He may have been, but he had not got the polish that so distinguished Fangio. I remember watching both of them in a certain corner in the Bari *grand prix*. Fangio would come around and just brush along the straw bales, not touching them, just alongside them, you know, beautiful. Ascari, when he came through, would just clip the kerb and straighten out, just a slight oversteer with power but every time he was just clipping the kerb. Fangio was on the identical line but he wasn't touching anything. I think that was about the extent of the difference, and it's a big difference.

"I wouldn't say anyone else was in Fangio's class. There were plenty of other *good* drivers. Jean Behra, on his day, was good. Musso, Castellotti, on their days. Portago had lasted long enough to get to be pretty good; I think Fon was a good driver, but I don't think he took things as seriously as he might have done. Motor-racing isn't quite the same thing as a run down the Cresta. Fon intended having fun. That was one of the reasons people liked him. He was always game for a lark. If he had lasted another couple of years . . .

"Ricardo Rodriguez probably needed only another year or two, then he should have had the judgement to match his ability. It was a pity Ricardo died. He was a nice man from a kind family. I think it wouldn't have happened on another circuit. The Mexico circuit was after all *his* course, he didn't like it that Surtees was quicker on it in practice. That was one thing. Another was that he had gone from driving Ferraris, basically under-steering cars, into a Lotus, which doesn't handle that way, and he hadn't given himself much time to get used to it. There seems to be little doubt that he was over his head, going too fast. There were competent observers there who told me so. But Ricardo was usually in a hurry. He seemed to be under psychological pressure.

"I wonder about Willy Mairesse sometimes. He runs pretty close to disaster, knowing that the disaster is there and maybe expecting that it may be there for him. Mairesse needs another year or two, and I hope he gives it to himself. He's a tiger.

"Giancarlo Baghetti is an intelligent driver. It's too early to say how good he is. He beat Dan Gurney at Rheims in 1961 by intelligence. He could keep up with Gurney, I wouldn't say he could outdrive him. I think Lorenzo Bandini is a better driver than Baghetti, I don't know how intelligent he is.

"I find Richie Ginther interesting. He's a Graham Hill type, a mechanic-driver. Good, too, competent, intelligent and safe. He can drive big cars and small cars and it doesn't matter much to him which. He knows his limitations and drives within them, he's not trying to prove he's the greatest. But he's that good anyway, he doesn't have to prove it.

"Ginther drove a beautiful race at Monte Carlo in 1961. Beautiful. He had the responsibility for his team there toward the end, for the first time, he was a new boy, and I thought he did a fantastic job actually. He kept the pressure on, I know I was trying damned hard and he was right behind me all the time. He never gave an inch. He didn't make an inch, but he never gave an inch, either.

"Masten Gregory is another who's come a long way," Moss said. "He used to be one of the hairiest drivers who ever sat in a motor-car. Do you remember how he used to jump out? Masten has leapt out of I don't know how many cars. When he got into trouble he would stand up and bail out, he's abandoned more than one car that looked to be on the wrong side of 100 miles an hour, too. But he doesn't do that any more. He's a conscientious and intelligent appraiser of the situation. He doesn't have to go in over his head any more. Remember, Masten Gregory has been in racing longer than anyone else who's now active, with the single exception of Maurice Trintignant. Think of that! He's dedicated now; I think he's a man who would do anything he felt was necessary in order to be better. I used to say to him: 'Masten, you're going to kill yourself.' Now I think it would have to be a case of very bad luck indeed to hurt Masten, I think he's come that far.

"I remember a time I think Masten would like to have run over me. It was in Havana, the year the Castro people kidnapped Fangio. There was a lot of oil on the circuit, and I let Masten past into first place, pretty heartlessly, rather like you'd send someone ahead of a squad of soldiers with a mine-detector. Let old Masten find the oil, I said to myself. Then there was a bad accident after a bit and a marshal put out a red flag. Masten stood on everything and slowed right down. I started to slow down, but then I ran through the regulations in my mind and remembered that a red flag, which meant everybody come to a grinding halt the race is over sort of thing, a red flag had no validity except when shown by the clerk of the course, usually at the finish-line. So I stuck it into second gear and jumped on the throttle and ran past Masten to win. That had been my intention anyway. But Masten was sore. He said he reckoned that he had really won the race, and that I had cheated him out of it. I said: 'If you don't know the regs, Masten, you must expect to be beaten by somebody who does.' But then I told him I'd split first prize money with him if he'd split second prize with me, so we came out dead even and then he felt better.

"Incidentally, the worst race in the world for rules is Le

Mans. If you memorize the Le Mans rules, boy, you've got
a head on your shoulders. And having them in your memory
doesn't mean they'll make sense.

"Most people who play games don't understand the rules.
I have a distinct philosophy about that. I think it's perfectly
all right to play so close to the rules that no one could get
a razor blade into the crack, but not to cheat. I mean, if
the regulations forbid alcohol fuel then nothing could make
me put a cupful of alcohol into a twenty-five-gallon tank of
petrol. But if the man who drew up the regulations *assumed,*
let's say, that everyone knew he meant 100-octane petrol,
and didn't specifically state as much, too bad, my car will
be set up for whatever fuel I please.

"One time at Monza I had something break on a Maserati,
the engine was running but the drive-shaft had gone. I
wanted to get to the pits pretty badly. A chap called Piotti
came up behind me, also driving a Maser, more or less on
the team, and I made great gesticulations and signals, telling
him to get in behind and push me. He did. I was waving
him on, faster, faster, and we got up to seventy-five or so
and then I waved him on past so he wouldn't get disqualified.
Now, all the pits could see was that I pulled in, presumably
under my own steam; after all, the engine was running and
I was going fast enough, with this idiot following much too
close. I wish I could remember if I shook my fist at him, I
hope I did, it would have been a nice touch. Anyway, my
point is, I think that was legal. The rule said: no outside
assistance. Well, now, is a team member an outsider? A
fine point.

"I'd do something like that for another driver, too. After
I'd won the G.P. of Portugal in 1958, I came around and
Mike Hawthorn had spun and stalled his engine. He was
trying to start it by pushing it up-hill, in the direction he'd

been going, and I shouted to him that he'd never get it going that way, to push it down-hill instead. Right, he finished second to me—without that second he wouldn't have been champion of the world, by the way—and when the officials wanted to disqualify him for pushing the car the wrong way to start it—against the traffic on the circuit—I prevented them, by testifying that while Mike had pushed the car counter-traffic, all right, he had not been *on* the actual circuit when he'd done it, and since the regulations didn't cover that point, he was within his rights. I said: 'After all, I was there and you gentlemen weren't.' I think that sort of thing is fair. Of course in 1960 my brakes locked and I went off the road at the same place. I tried the push-start I'd told Mike to use, but they disqualified me.

"Another time I noticed that on a certain circuit I needed to use about a foot, just about twelve inches of the pull-off zone for coming into the pits, if I wanted to go really and truly fast through a bend. So, knowing I could do it only once and get away with it, I waited until I needed one really quick lap, and I came through that bend flat out in third gear I believe it was, and I took the extra foot; and immediately I put my hand out, I made a signal that I was coming into the pits, I fiddled with the gear-lever, not lifting off on the throttle, not a bit of it, but pretending to pull and tug a little as though it was jammed, and then just as I knew I was flat-out in that gear, hadn't a rev left to get, I pulled my hand in, shoved the thing into the next gear, waved to my pit that I was okay now, I had got the stuck gear-lever freed. I could think of a good many things like that one can do.

"Some regulations are silly, and should be publicly mocked, for the good of the sport. For example, at Monza in 1962 they were concerned about the bad accident in 1961, when Taffy von Trips was killed, and they decided to narrow the track, which was perfectly silly, and to do this they put a row of cones opposite the pits. And they said: 'If you touch a cone you are out of the race, because they represent a concrete wall.' Can you imagine such nonsense? Of course, for real raving nonsense, Monza is the place. Every year you'll see some photographer, with press passes all over him, taking a picture and next thing a couple of *polizia* will be dragging him screaming off to the dungeon or whatever. They don't care what kind of passes you've got.

"Anyway, Graham Hill won at Monza in 1962, and I reckon it would have been nice if he'd come around, after he'd taken the flag, and was officially the winner and they couldn't do anything to him, it would have been nice if he'd gone along the line of cones and picked up the first one and put it on the second, and those on the third, and so on until at the end he was standing up in his car and making a farce of the whole damned thing. Of course that sort of thing isn't in Graham's nature, and that's nothing against him, he's not the type. For a job like that you want someone like, say, Duncan Hamilton. Hamilton would probably have picked the cones up and thrown them into the crowd for souvenirs. Or he'd have called a cop over and put a cone on his head for a hat."

"Stirling, you know the tired old question, if you had a son. . . ."

"Yes. Would I want him to be a driver? I would suggest to him that if he didn't want to do it so badly he couldn't think of anything else, he should try to put it out of his mind. Having said that, I believe I'd do what my father did: he didn't forbid me, he didn't urge me to do it, and when I'd started he never told me to try harder, to go faster, to extend myself. He made the right decision, I think, and so did I. Motor-racing has given me a wonderful life. I've seen the world, I've met hundreds of interesting and pleasant people I shouldn't have known otherwise, I've made a good deal of money, and, most of all, I have enjoyed myself. I've been down some of the time, right, but I've been up much more of the time, sometimes I think I've had two lifetimes full of fun, and I'm not yet thirty-five."

"And you have no regrets?"

"Not one. I regret nothing. Nothing. Nothing!"

CHAPTER V

"Not only ought Fortune to be pictured on a
wheel, but everything else in the world."

George Herbert

CHAPTER V

KATHARINE STUART MOLSON and Stirling Craufurd Moss were married in St. Peter's, Eaton Square, London, on October 7, 1957. Ken Gregory was best man. Margot Beaubien was chief bridesmaid. Peter Collins and Mike Hawthorn, among others, were ushers. The new Mr. and Mrs. Moss spent their honeymoon in Amsterdam.

They had met, casually, in Nassau in 1951, and again during the 1956 running of Le Mans. They were deeply in love when they married. They separated in two years, and began divorce proceedings soon afterwards. Parting was a heavy blow for each of them, and they have not wholly recovered from it. Their marriage was probably a typical case-history of failure caused by too much career and too little experience.

"We had a lot in common," Stirling says, "but we were immature. I'm obviously not qualified to say what the trouble was. I know that one problem was that Katie had been brought up in a family that was very wealthy and when we were married I said: 'Now look, you've got money of your own, fair enough, but you jolly well start a trust, your money is to go there, perhaps for our children, or whatever you like—but I pay the bills. And I did.'

"Not that I was big about it, I wasn't, sometimes I looked like a cheapskate. When Katie wanted a maid, I said: 'Well, you're not having a maid.' She said: 'Why not, I want a maid.' I just said no. I was trying to run her life, I didn't want her to have the whole day free, just to be idle. I just didn't want her hanging about with nothing to do. And of course Katie's friends were inclined to say to her: 'Look here, that's pretty cheap of him, why doesn't he let you have a maid, it's only three pounds a week or something.' But it wasn't the three pounds, or five or whatever, it was the principle of the thing, and maybe I was wrong-headed and stubborn.

"We did have money trouble, which, looking back on it, I suppose was truly absurd and juvenile because after all there was plenty of the stuff about. But I gave Katie an allowance, she could do what she wanted with it, but if she wanted to buy a dress that was over her allowance, well, she couldn't. I'm sure I went too far with the whole idea, and it was a bad idea to begin with. I rather think it's silly, now, for any man to be bothered by the fact that the woman he marries has a great deal of money—but that's now, and we're talking about 1957, and, you'd better believe it, 1957 looks a long way off.

"I tried to get Katie to start a little shop, to have some interest. I wanted her to *do* more. Clear enough, now, that was Stirling Moss of Stirling Moss Limited saying: 'Come on, here's an entire hour and a half to put something into, let's get cracking'—that was me, I was on the jump so everybody else had to be; all right, I see it now, I didn't then.

"Another mistake I made, and Katie agreed when I asked her just the other day, and that was that I never made her feel really wanted. Certainly that is one thing a man should do. Now, it happens that I'm very much self-supporting. I don't mean financially, of course. I mean that I try to take care of myself. I want to be my own man. I let Katie see this too clearly. She obviously felt, what does he need me for? For decoration? For sex? I didn't make her feel

needed as much as I should have done. If we'd had a child
. . . but that's begging the issue. The irony of it was that
I knew I needed her, and badly, but I just had not got the
capability to explain it to her. It was an impasse. It was the
old story: immaturity, inexperience, failure in simple communication between two people.

"Then there was the pressure of motor-racing. In the
first place, we had little privacy. I was living in a suitcase
and in my office and at race-meetings, and that kind of
thing is hard for a woman to accept. And I've had reporters
phone me at 3 o'clock in the morning many times, often for
quite a trivial reason. I've had reporters call me on the radio
at 4 a.m. in the Australian bush. I've been called at 6 a.m.
in Bangkok to take a call from London—and in Bangkok
you don't just pick up the telephone, you have to go to the
central post office to answer.

"Then, a woman doesn't like being put on exhibition
every time she goes out for a drink or to the theatre. Oh,
perhaps some women do, real career women, actresses most
of course, but Katie didn't, I know that.

"We decided at the beginning that Katie should come to
races with me, that that would be better than staying at
home and waiting to hear. Even that may have been wrong,
because the strain of racing is terrible for those who *watch*.
It makes me very nervous to watch my sister Pat drive in
competition, and by God I know that if I had to go to a
circuit and sit down and watch her in a flat-out Formula
race—well, I just wouldn't go, that's all. I wouldn't go.
And Katie more or less had to go.

"Unless one's been concerned with someone who's running in a motor-race, it's hard to understand what a strain
it can be. I'm convinced that much of the strain lies in the
regularity of any one driver's appearance. You're in the

pit, let's say, and it's your brother driving, and here you have a lap-chart going, and a split-second watch, and every 4 minutes 10 seconds your brother comes by, let's say he's a good driver and settled down, and he stays on the pace within a few seconds. This goes on for an hour, and then suddenly, 4.10 comes, 4.12, 4.15 and he doesn't come past, 4.20, 4.25, believe me, you don't even hear the racket of other cars passing, there's such a silence because you can't hear the one engine you're waiting for, and every second that ticks off sounds like Big Ben to you. And no matter how well disciplined you are, you'll think of all the people you used to know who're not with us any more, and what happened to them, and it's very rough . . . well, you know well enough how it is, Ken. And certainly this is a hard thing for one's wife to take; it was for Katie. You told me you were near Katie one day when I didn't come around, and that she went white. . . ."

[Stirling had run out of fuel on the far side of the circuit. He had had his foot hard down the last time he'd gone by and when he didn't come around, someone near the pit loudly expressed the opinion that he'd had a shunt. Some minutes passed, probably only five or six—but that can seem very many—before word came through that he was un-hurt and walking back. He came the quickest way, cross-country, and the sun on his white overalls identified him a long way off. Katie Moss went to meet him, and as they approached, each headed a small, growing wedge-shaped mob of the curious. Katie ran the last few steps and they kissed but the sensation must have been some-thing like making love under a spot-light, and they walked quickly and soberly back to the pit, their two crowds, now massed into one, hustling idiotically along behind them.]

126

"So there was that, and who knows how many other things? I was in South America, I was on my way back to pick her up in Nassau, we had a pleasant house we'd built in Nassau, and a friend met me and said: 'Katie says, look, better if you don't come back sort of thing, and this is it, finally'—and that was that.

"Katie for me had a great appeal. She was a tomboy on the one hand and a lady on the other and sexy in both roles; she could be out with an engine-fitter or Lord So-and-so and get along equally well with them and if I were with you and you'd brought your wife I'd know jolly well your wife would be entertained if you and I wanted to talk together. She was most adaptable; she was a good cook, she was a very good driver. We enjoyed a lot of things together, water-ski-ing, cinema, we liked the same sort of theatre. Katie's taste was different from mine and she was strong enough, if you like, to change my taste in many things, in the way I dress and so on. She even changed my taste in colours, she changed my attitude toward colour. Now I look at my house and it's amusing, the place looks as if I'd designed it for Katie; actually I didn't, it's designed as *I* like it, only what I like now is rather what she made me like, or led me to like would be a more nearly accurate way to put it. I know I never thought, planning a room or anything, Katie would like that, because it's too late for that and I know it and I feel it.

"At the root of it, I say motor-racing was responsible for the failure of our marriage. The other things that contributed, the inexperience, the immaturity, were things that grew out of motor-racing, rather, they resulted from my obsession with it. I'm not in the least bitter, you know that. I took a very great deal out of motor-racing, but I put a lot back, too, I do feel that I gave it all but my life. Very well,

I didn't have to do. I think that if a driver is prepared to be Number Two, is willing to be Number Two, then I think that motor-racing is a pleasant life, indeed, an easy life, but if one's not prepared to be Number Two, if one won't settle for that . . . then, it's hard. Katie was everything to me. I was shattered when we parted. I very nearly came unstuck, and I tried hard to get her back.

"We didn't part as sharply as I may have made it sound, a minute ago. We knew in December of 1959, all right, but for various reasons that seemed valid at the time we felt we had to keep it a secret until after the New Year. Actually it wasn't announced until March 17, and during all that time from December we lived together, but not really, we weren't lovers. Looking back, we certainly didn't make it easy for ourselves, staying together, and even sleeping together. I remember going over to Puerto Rico when Katie was skeet-shooting there, she was a damned good shot, and I had sort of to peck her on the cheek and say 'Good-night and I hope you do well tomorrow, darling, good luck'—and then turn over and try to think of something that would knock me out and put me to sleep. And just recently, just the other day, I saw Katie and I said to her: 'Look, did you know what I was going through in those times?' and do you know, she didn't? So at least I was a good actor. I was determined I wouldn't let her know how much it really upset me, my pride wouldn't allow it.

"When I was hurt at Spa, Katie said she would come to London from Nassau if I wanted her to, and I desperately did want her to, but I said no, I didn't want her to come just because she felt sorry for me.

"In March we separated. I remember you've written somewhere that in this time of stress I missed no motor-races, and some people might think that was callous of me,

'Attitude,' or position of the car in the classic
four-wheel drift—a perfect example.

The Moss wave of thanks.
The car he is passing is off the picture to the left.

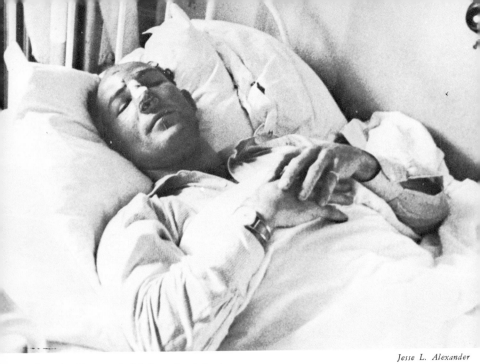

Jesse L. Alexander

After the Spa crash, his legs, back broken.

At Goodwood, rescuers cut the car up.

Daily Mail

A happier ending: Moss after a 1961 event
in which he had lapped all but two drivers.

Jesse L. Alexander

With Katie Molson Moss after he had won the Italian *Grand Prix* at Monza.
The year, 1956.

The tight fit, the tiny wheel of modern *grand prix* cars,
Moss just before the Goodwood crash.

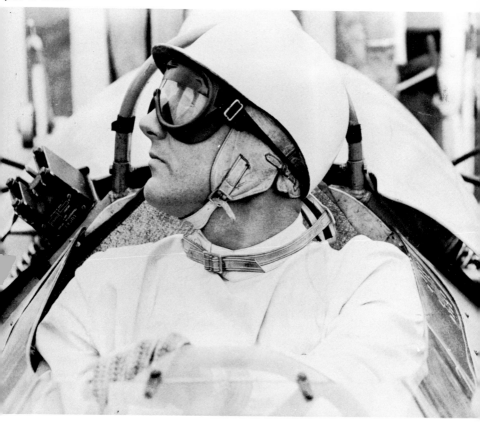

Water skiing,
Acapulco,
Mexico

Associated Press Phot

Jesse L. Alexander

A typical **G.P.** circuit: Spa, in Belgium.

The last time around: May 1, 1963, Moss running alone on the
Goodwood race-course.

but it wasn't. This whole lump of mud and rock and molten nickel or whatever it is that we're living on is turning a thousand miles an hour and is good for another five billion years or so, and that's what governs us: life is moving, and if you don't keep on moving . . . Jean Behra used to say, when people talked to him about how one might be killed motor-racing, going so fast, Jean would say: '*Alors,* those ones who are not moving, they are dead already, isn't that true?'

"I felt like crawling into a cave, but I stayed out of it. I kept on motor-racing. I told myself: 'Right, you're not dead, so you're not going to act as if you were. Go out and live it up.' The old story: after the crash, go back up in the airplane. As you've said: back up on the high wire.

"I started going out. I didn't really want to. It was a long time after the separation before I could even contemplate going to bed with a girl. And then, when I tried, I was ineffective. I know the medical people say that any man who denies this has happened to him is a liar, but it was the first time it had happened to me, or anything like it, and it was a terrible jolt. I went to a psychiatrist about it. Of course, one would hardly need a printed diagram to know what was happening, it was simply that I didn't *want* anybody else, I was forcing myself, and my subconscious mind or whatever was saying: 'No, you don't, mate, you're just not in charge here.' Well, when I understood what was happening, I got back in charge.

"Now, these years later, I am staggered at seeing what time will do. The attempts I made to get Katie back hardly seem a reality, and I think of her as one of my best friends. Some people find it hard to believe that Katie and I are such close friends. But after all, about five years ago I married the person I considered my ideal. I'm fickle—but I'm not that changeable! Katie and I still have a great deal in common. I keep her picture in my room, perhaps because she is my friend, perhaps to remind me to try to be more realistic and intelligent next time, if there is a next time, perhaps for some other reason. If I knew I would say. I don't know."

CHAPTER VI

"In all games, it is good to end a winner."
Thomas Fuller

"**N**O ONE ever offered me a shilling to let someone else win a race," Stirling Moss said, "and I've not heard of any such thing being done, in my time. Certainly drivers in the same team have let other drivers pass, and that sort of thing, and have boxed-off cars, but on orders, not for money. A famous example of that, I suppose, was the *Grand Prix* of Morocco in 1958, when the championship of the world hung between me and Mike Hawthorn. To take the championship I had to win the race and have as well the extra point for making fastest lap, whereas Mike had only to take second place. I made fastest lap, and I won the race by more than a minute, but Mike was champion, because Phil Hill, his team-mate, lying second, dropped back to third. One might say that it was Phil who beat me, not Mike, but I've never felt a trace of bitterness against Phil for it—if he hadn't done it, he'd have been fired off the Ferrari team five seconds after he stepped out of the motorcar. Ideally, of course, every driver would try his best all the time, but that's not the way things are done.

"Some people like to say that motor-racing is the cleanest game in the world, the cleanest sport. The older I get, the more I distrust absolutes like that, but it is a clean sport, and to me it's a saintly sport compared with any other.

"That's not to say that there hasn't been crookedness, that there haven't been fixed races. I'm sure there must have been. We know, for instance, that the Grand Prix of Tripoli in 1933 was, as they say in the States, a boat-race, a tank-job. And, unhappily, there were a lot of important people running in that race: Nuvolari, Varzi, Borzacchini, Campari, Birkin, Fagioli.

"There was a lottery on the Tripoli G.P. You must remember that this was in Mussolini's time. People always say that it was Hitler who first really exploited motor-racing as a national policy, as propaganda, but in fact Mussolini did it first. Marshal Balbo was running the Tripoli race. I've forgotten what the lottery prize was in *lire* but it was £80,000 and in those days I believe the pound was worth twice what it is today, so the winner of the lottery stood to collect a major fortune.

"A ticket-holder—we'll call him Giovanni—drew Achille Varzi to win the race and he went around to see him. Giovanni told Varzi that if he could persuade the other drivers to be sure that he won, he, Giovanni, would give him half his winnings. 'Right,' Varzi said, 'fair enough, but how can I be sure?' So Giovanni gave him a written agreement! Then, presumably, Varzi went around to talk to the other drivers.

"Apparently it was a neat arrangement but unfortunately one little thing went wrong: Varzi fouled a couple of plugs when he was lying third, and just beginning to close up on the leaders. This made things difficult for everybody, the drivers behind him as well as those in front. Campari just went into the pits and stayed there. Borzacchini somehow ran into an oil-drum and blew a tyre. Nuvolari coasted to a stop at the head of the straight, half-a-minute in the lead, and made a big show of pointing to his tank, and screaming that he was out of petrol. A mechanic had to come running with a churn to get him going again, and Varzi just pipped him to win, limping along on six cylinders. But it was a bit plain that something had been afoot and there was a scandal. Nothing happened to the drivers, there were too many of them and they were too important —but the lottery-rules were changed. After that, the winning tickets were not drawn until five minutes before the off!

"People have suggested to me that if motor-racing were a betting game, like horse-racing, there would be a good deal of hanky-panky. I doubt it. I suppose it's easier to sabotage a racing-car than it is to dope a horse, but I doubt if it would be as effective. If you dope a horse he will just run faster, or slower, depending upon what you've given him; but anything that's done to sabotage a racing-car carries the risk of putting it out of control, and that means that other cars may be involved. If someone, let us say, gets half-a-pint of sugar syrup into my petrol-tank, just when my engine seizes solid I may be passing the car he hopes will win, and perhaps it goes out of the race with me.

"If you did it the other way, by bribery, I think you would have to spend a great deal of money and buy *all* the drivers, because with competition the way it is today you couldn't buy just the top two or three. There are, I would reckon, six top drivers who are pretty close; after that you get another six or so who are pretty terrific as well. I wouldn't put Innes Ireland or Jo Bonnier in the first six, but they're that good that you couldn't afford to back off much, boy, before they'd be worrying you. Even after that lot you come to another group of perhaps six who are pretty darned good. They wouldn't beat Graham Hill, they wouldn't beat Dan Gurney, no, but I can tell you that Graham or Dan couldn't go to sleep for long before they *would* be beaten. You'd have to buy the whole field, which is what I presume happened at Tripoli, from reading Neubauer's account of it. I imagine one or two of the drivers went along without taking any money, just not to spoil the pitch for the others. But trying to buy the field today would be an impractical solution because you wouldn't have that much money and because there are some people whom you simply couldn't buy for any amount of money. I would say the whole list of 1963 ranked drivers couldn't be bought. I think some of them would not only refuse, they might react in an unpleasant fashion. I shouldn't think it would be wise to try such a proposition on Jo Bonnier, for example. Or Innes Ireland. Innes just might call you a bloody some-thing-or-other and pop you one."

"He'll call you a bloody something-or-other in the friend-liest way," I said. "When I first met Ireland, at Watkins Glen, he pointed a finger at me and he said: 'I know you! When I saw you this morning I said to somebody: "I know the bloody man, I saw him on the bloody telly in the bloody motel last night!"'"

"I can hear him now," Stirling said. "He's got a bloody big voice, Innes. But to go back, isn't it true that the sports in which bribery and fixing are common are games like horse-racing and dog-racing, where the lives of the players aren't at stake?"

"I don't think so," I said. "I think that the governing factor is money, and I think that mountain-climbing, which kills 300-odd people in the average year, and tiddley-winks, which I hope I'm right in saying has yet to produce its first fatality, would both be crooked if there was money in them. After all, boxing, at least in the United States, where it's biggest, and where most championships are decided, is very dirty—and boxing is dangerous. About the same num-ber of men have been killed since the war in boxing as in motor-racing, 175–180, although out of a very much bigger total of participants."

136

"It's still not really a parallel with motor-racing, though, is it," Stirling said.

"No," I said. "But I don't know what *is* a parallel, unless it was chariot-racing in the Roman Empire, and I'm sure there were plenty of fixed chariot-races, because there were vast sums of money bet, and big purses for the drivers. Daniel Mannix, a friend of mine who knows a great deal about it, has written that a top driver could make a hundred times the salary of a Roman senator, and the man who was probably the greatest charioteer of all time, an ex-Spanish slave named Diocles—a medium-height dark-haired man, by the way—was worth about 750,000 1963 pounds sterling when he retired. Diocles once won a race for a side-bet of more than £25,000. The bet had been that he couldn't win driving a four-horse hitch without a whip. The whip wasn't used to beat the horses, it was a guide. The drivers used the reins for coarse steering, so to speak, but when it got down to inches, they held the whip against one or the other shoulders of the lead horse, as a signal."

"Sounds very dodgey," Stirling said.

"Yes, I think it must have been."

"I wouldn't want anything to do with a big betting sport," Stirling said, "though I don't care how much the participants get, they're making the effort, they're doing the entertaining, they're taking the risk, fair enough, and good luck to them. And I agree with you, betting does always carry with it at least the risk of corruption. But you don't need betting to attract big crowds. In Europe I should think football was the biggest spectator sport and it's not a big betting game, because the pools are really a form of lottery, the odds are so high; then comes horse-racing, I suppose that's the biggest of all betting games; and then motor-racing, with no betting at all. And in the States it's horse-racing first, motor-racing second, then baseball and football and basketball and that lot, right?"

"Yes. Motor-racing is the second biggest American spectator sport."

"And there isn't a dollar bet on it, is there, even at Indianapolis?"

"No. Perhaps a few private bets."

"I believe there used to be a bit of betting on British races, before the war. I'm told there were bookmakers at Donington, when the Germans came over in 1938. The bookmakers didn't know anything about form, and they posted long odds against the Auto-Unions and the Mercs, which, of course, came in one-two-three. They couldn't pay off."

"Stirling, I used to know a journalist—he worked for me for a long time when I was an editor—who specialized in turning up corruption in government and financial circles all over the world. He was very able and very tough-minded. I knew he'd been threatened on the one hand and offered bribes on the other, and I said to him one day: 'Look here, everyone has a price, and what is yours, you should have been either dead or rich years ago.' And he said: 'It would have to be enough so that I'd never need to work again and, in addition, enough to compensate me for the enjoyment I get out of working, because, don't you see, the first dollar I took would destroy me, I never could work again.'"

"I wouldn't know how to put it better," Stirling said. "If someone came to me, someone I knew was worth millions, and said, here's a signed cheque, fill it in as you please—but don't win tomorrow, I couldn't do it, not because I'm a saint, not because I'm incorruptible, I doubt I am, but because he'd be putting me out of motor-racing. He'd be buying my life, and there isn't that much money."

CHAPTER VII

"Death is like furniture in a familiar room. He knows it is there but he hasn't noticed it in a long time."

Robert Daley

CHAPTER VII

" Grand prix racing is much more of an art now than a matter of survival of the fittest," Moss says. "I can't think of anyone who races every week who thinks it's his bravery that gets him through. Bravery is common. In 1954, I think it was, some 4,000 people wrote to Mercedes-Benz asking for a place on the team. They all thought they were brave enough for the job, and I daresay five hundred or so of them would have been. Bravery isn't hard to find. Skill is something else again. Drivers who have *only* courage don't drive for long.

"I would say courage comes into the equation, oh, let's say you're driving a car belonging to a team and a wheel falls off a team-mate's car and you see it at the side of the road and you have to keep going, in a sister-car, identical. That takes a certain amount of courage. You have an intellectually valid reason for suspicion: if it was a design-error that knocked the wheel off his car, the same thing can happen to yours.

"On the other hand, if a wheel came off my car today in practice or I had a brake failure in practice and nothing was broken on the car or on myself, in other words, if I got away with it, I could get into that car as soon as you could change the wheel or put the brakes right and go straight out and not worry at all—*at all*. It is a complete blanking of the mind, it isn't courage, it's absolute control of the mind. I say to myself, there's no use thinking about it, so I shan't, and I don't.

141

"I've had plenty of wheels come off and I'm damned sure I know why: I go through the corners a bit faster than the next bloke and doing that I put a greater G-loading through the suspension.* The designer of the car may say: 'Right, we can get one G stopping force and point eight G cornering and that's the lot. Well, I know jolly well, boy, I can get one G stopping together with point eight G cornering, together with a bump, and it will add up to two or perhaps three G in that corner. The designer will tell you that you can't, the tyre-adhesion factor won't let you, the tyres will let go and the car will slide before the force reaches that many G's, but nevertheless you can. I've had enough wheels come off to know. I've had wheels come off and brakes fail and steering-gear collapse and gearboxes break up, I've had more gearboxes break than most people have had in their cars and I've had my experience to protect me in what people say is a dangerous sport. But do you know one thing I would not do, Ken? I would not go up on a thirty-foot board and dive. And yet I know as well as you do, boy, that if it's deep enough water I'm not going to hurt m'self, but I just haven't got the guts to do it. I would hold my nose and I would jump.

"It took courage as far as I was concerned to do the record attempts with the M.G. on the salt-flats in Utah in 1957, mainly because they buttoned me into the thing and I knew it took three miles to stop it and there wasn't a hope in hell of getting out of it if it caught fire. That I didn't like. I had quite a long time to think about it, while the thing was building up to 100, 150, 200, 250 miles an hour, and the whole situation was made worse by the fact that when you'd gone through the measured mile you cut

* "G" is a symbol for gravity. A car turning a corner fast enough to produce a force of two G is exerting a sidewise force equal to twice its weight.

the ignition and put your foot flat down to suck any flames through the engine and out the pipe and when you did that you got a smell of fuel, of fumes throughout the car . . . you wouldn't get out because to start with, the lid came down from the front, you know wind-pressure would hold the nose down even if you could undo it; there was a release inside, but if the thing went on fire you'd be all thumbs. The runs turned out well, though, and I set up five records.

"I've been truly frightened twice, or perhaps I should say, the two times I was most frightened were at Monza in 1958 and Spa in 1960. At Monza I was doing 160 miles an hour or so in a Maserati, when the steering sheared on the banking, the wheel just came loose in my hands, it was no longer connected to anything. I had time to think about it, to try to find something to do, but there was nothing for it, I stood on the brakes, which were nothing, they were sports-car brakes, you couldn't even feel them bite at that speed, then I thought maybe I could steer it by holding the bare steering-shaft between my feet, which was silly, of course, but gives you an idea how bad the situation really was; I knew I just had to sit and wait and I knew damned well I had to be killed. I was sure we were going over the top of the banking. I ripped steel posts out of the concrete for more than fifty yards. That car slid for a quarter of a mile, blowing its tyres, buckling the wheels, breaking itself up . . . when it stopped, and right side up, I was surprised to find myself alive, I can tell you that. I could hardly believe it.

"The other time was when the wheel came off in Belgium. I was doing perhaps 140 miles an hour when the car suddenly went into a very violent oversteer condition. First I thought I had hit oil, then I saw the wheel go past me. I knew I was going to crash, I jumped on the brakes and tried to spin the car around. It's best to hit going backward, it distributes the shock more evenly over your body. Also, you can't see what you're going to hit! I took fifty miles an hour off it before I hit. I hung on, you'd better believe I hung on, until I felt the tail start to come up, I knew the car was going over, so I let go the wheel, I'd already bent it to a pretzel, I let myself go limp and I went out. Next thing I knew, I was on my hands and knees beside the road and I couldn't see and I couldn't breathe. And *that* frightened me. I was in great pain around my chest, and I was afraid I had broken ribs and that they would puncture my heart or my lungs. That was how Bobby Baird died, at Snetterton in 1953. He got up and walked around after the crash and then he died. I was more afraid of that happening than I was when I knew I was going to hit that bank at around a hundred miles an hour.

"I had myself fairly well in hand, but I did do one bad thing; other drivers kept running up, of course, Bruce McLaren and Graham Hill and Phil Hill and others, and I asked someone, I think it was Bruce, to help me breathe by giving me artificial respiration. I was confused. He wouldn't do it, and of course he was dead right not to, because I could have had broken ribs. In fact, my back was broken with three crushed vertebrae.

"At Goodwood, I suppose I must have been frightened, but since I don't remember even getting out of bed that day. . . .

"When I did the Portuguese G.P., a couple of months after the Spa crash, I remember feeling some fear. I was driving the same type of car I'd crashed at Spa, and that circuit is tree-lined and I remember going through a really fast corner, 130 miles an hour or something like that and the idea flashed through my mind, what would happen if a wheel came off *here*? All one can really do is put it out of one's mind. One's just got to conquer that. It isn't courage, it's just a case of overcoming whatever it is that worries you.

"People think courage is required for things that don't need it at all. For example, people say to me: 'How do you dare take your hands off the wheel to wave to someone in a corner'—maybe they've heard me lecturing on the subject of one-hand driving on the road, which I think is so stupid! What they don't know, is that once a car is presented to a corner, other things being equal, that is, no oil on the track or something funny happening, that car has a sort of line of destiny—a line on which the damned thing is going to go no matter what; once a car has been set up for a corner, it should hold its line at the driver's will. That is one of the primary techniques of high-speed driving. I remember doing a demonstration in a Healey, in about a ninety-mile-an-hour wide right-hand sweep, where I started on the left, set the car up and then told the student to watch the steering wheel, and I would go from the very left verge, clip within a couple of inches of the apex of the bend and go out the exit to the very verge within say three or four inches, without moving the steering wheel a fraction of an inch over, say, two hundred and fifty yards. Of course, you do compromise with the throttle, but I think once you've got it set up, you should be able to go to nine-tenths motoring anyway. It's only when you're right on the ragged edge, at ten-tenths, that you do need quite a lot of steering to keep the thing exactly in balance, but one doesn't go beyond nine-tenths all that frequently. And so, once you've got the thing set up, you can let go with one hand or the other, it doesn't make any difference, the decision has been taken.

[A racing car, at racing speeds, spends quite a lot of time going sideways, 'drifting' as it's called, with all four wheels sliding equally. This is generally held to be the fastest way through a bend, although there is some indication that modern suspensions are altering the picture. When the car is going fast enough, and it must be going very fast if the road is dry, the driver can provoke a drift by turning the steering wheel sharply and abruptly—but always smoothly—and by hitting the brakes hard, once. The car's adhesion to the road is broken, and it is thereafter steered with the throttle, more throttle increasing the angle of slide, usually mis-called a drift, the nose pointing to the inside of the bend, and less throttle decreasing it, because the faster the rear tyres are *spinning* on the road, the less grip they have. Going through a series of S-bends very fast, a driver can be extremely busy with the steering wheel, and a layman sitting beside him would be quite unable to tell what he was doing. He would be altering not so much the *direction* of the car, in the sense of steering the front of it, as altering the whole attitude of the car relative to the road, pointing it now this way and now that—in various sliding positions; braking and restoring adhesion of the front wheels separately, the rear wheels separately, or all four together. Going through a long S-bend at say 125 miles an hour, a driver of Moss's calibre might change the whole direction in which the car is pointing on the road as many as six times. Maintenance of inch-by-inch control of a car doing perhaps 150 miles an hour partially forward and partially sideways is the essence of the difference between race-driving and ordinary driving. It is a skill difficult to acquire, since it can't be learned with the car going at a safe slow speed. Also, the sudden appearance of a patch of oil, sand, or a puddle of water can fatally upset the requisite balance.]

Tazio Nuvolari is said to have contributed to racing the idea of the controlled four-wheel drift; Moss brought to it a radical concept of braking. It has from the beginning, since the pioneer days when a skid was referred to as 'the dread side-slip', been held basic to the driving of any motor-car, passenger or racing, that the brakes should never be applied in a corner. Brake before the corner, accelerate coming out of it, is holy writ. Braking whilst actually in the corner was supposed to bring automatic disaster—and it did often seem to do. Moss upset all that. He applied brakes when the car was in the actual corner, turning, and then instantly banged on full acceleration, so that the car was always under either heavy braking or severe acceleration, and spent no time coasting. The difference between this technique and the old one can amount to useful fractions of seconds, and in the frantic world of *grand prix* racing, a tenth of a second in each of ten corners can make the difference between losing and winning, or between winning desperately or winning almost easily. Of course, taking one tenth-second too much off a corner can bring disaster.

Moss's attention to the details, the *minutiae* of motor-racing has been matched by very few drivers indeed. Off-hand I would say only by Piero Taruffi and by Tazio Nuvolari. The attention he has given to the 'Le Mans' start is an example. In this method of beginning a race, the drivers stand across the track from their parked cars. At flag-fall, they run to them, jump in, start the engines and go. It is used in very few races. Watching any Le Mans-type start, it was always easy to spot Moss. He was the one in a sprinter's crouch. He had practised. Almost invariably, he was first to the car, first to have the engine going, and first away. Really earnest drivers watched Moss, not the starter's flag. Hours of practising this little-used device seemed a waste of time to most drivers. It's used only in long-distance races. What's the point in getting to be expert in something that will save a maximum, say, of two seconds in a 24-hour race? Moss wasn't interested in the two seconds at all. He became the fastest Le Mans starter in the business in order to have a clear track for the first lap; to get well away, and to avoid the possible disaster that always lurks in a traffic-jam of forty or fifty cars, not by any means all of them in the hands of front-rank experts, running flat-out for the first corner, with a shunt always possible.

Stirling's determination in the matter was notorious among other drivers, of course. As a gag, Mike Hawthorn once blatantly and openly jumped the gun, starting to run well before the flag fell. The dead hush that always marks a Le Mans start at a big race was ripped by Moss's furious and despairing shout: "Mike, you bastard!"

Reeling with laughter, Hawthorn could barely start his own car, and got away well behind the leaders.

"If, for example, a four-wheel slide gets out of hand," Moss says, "the driver senses the loss of the vehicle, before it becomes apparent to anyone else, through the steering wheel. It's a funny thing, it's practically a noise. When you lose the back-end of a car you just feel it go. When you lose the front-end you feel a 'growl' through the steering wheel. You hear a sort of rumble. There *can't* be any sound, you'd never hear any sound, you're wearing ear-plugs and the engine is screaming away just behind your head, but I can assure you that you nearly hear this sensation, this growling, rumbling sound as the thing is losing adhesion. When you lose the whole bloody vehicle you don't get either of these sensations, I suppose the two just cancel each other out, you just know the car is moving sideways more than it should be at that moment; say it's moving eight feet sideways per eighty feet forward, and that may be exactly what you want, but if the rate rises to nine feet sideways per eighty feet forward you know somewhere inside you that this is not right, and if you worked out the equation quickly enough, you know there's not going to be enough road. . . . I wish I could explain that phenomenon of the noise better, I cannot. I don't suppose I really hear it. I sense it, somehow."

[Alf Francis has said that Moss clearly has an inexplicable anticipatory sense, and that he many times saved himself serious trouble by stopping just *before* a rear axle let go, just before a wheel-bearing locked up. Francis has also recorded his belief that an elementary telepathic communication sometimes existed between him and Moss *when Moss was driving*. (Underlining mine.) To persons familiar with telepathic phenomena, the distinction is significant. Telepathy, which of course clearly does exist, though little understood, is most likely to occur under conditions of intense concentration and personal involvement, and although he has watched so many hundreds of races, Francis, unlike many mechanics, still finds the spectacle absolutely compelling and exciting. In assessing these rather esoteric opinions of Alf Francis, it is important to know that he is a hard-headed, practical, sceptical and independent personality.]

"I think one must have these extra sensibilities if one's to go on a long time," Moss says. "Perhaps one's born with some of them, unusually acute vision, for instance, but I think most of them are the result of the endless polishing and honing, through experience, of quite ordinary abilities. I have said before: I think a man can do anything he really wants to do. And I suppose one *must,* for safety's sake, be afraid of some things. You know, Dick Seaman died at Spa in 1939 not because he was so badly hurt in the crash, but because he sat in the car *after* the crash, until it began to burn. Seaman died of burns. I pounded that into my head, you'd better believe I did, until I had come to the point where my subconscious could take over, if I had been too badly hurt to think. I had that in hand as early as 1950. In the Naples G.P. that year a fellow burst my front tyre and put me off the road into a tree. I had some teeth knocked out, and my knee was broken, and I was dazed, but the instant my car—it was an H.W.M.—had stopped, I was out of it and running, broken knee or no broken knee, and I went a good way, too."

[Said Geoffrey Dupree, the course marshal who was the first man to reach Moss at Goodwood: "He was totally unconscious, but his body was shifting and moving and struggling, trying to leave the car."]

"One's entitled to be afraid of something like that. I'm not sure whether I am more afraid of burning, or dying, or if it's the *needlessness* of dying because you haven't taken the trouble to think ahead a little bit.

"One *must* be afraid of some things. After I'd got out of the Atkinson Morley Hospital, after the Goodwood shunt, I was euphoric, which as you know is a kind of unreal sense of well-being. You noticed it in the hospital, you wrote that I couldn't stop talking. Now, euphoria, if it goes far enough, can be very dangerous, because you can walk across Piccadilly Circus at high noon perfectly convinced that nothing can touch you; you can walk on the ledge of a building and be sure you won't fall off; all natural fears have been taken from you. I tried hard to get over that. Of course part of it was because my brain had been injured, nothing I could do about *that* until it healed itself. But I tried hard to understand what was happening to me. One of the nurses was very helpful to me about all that. You met her, Christine Williams. She knew a lot about neurological things, she brought me books and medical journals and helped me to plough through them. If you're really euphoric, you're fearless. And if you're fearless, you'll kill yourself, just walking about, never mind motor-racing.

"Fear is always there and we must control it. For example, I will not sit on the pit-counter, and look at my car standing on the grid, and say to myself, that front wheel hub-nut might be loose, so I shall just stroll over and tap it with a hammer. Once I start doing that I shall have to strip the car myself, before every race. I have never gone around a car that Alf Francis had prepared to check things like that. Never! I would think that a ridiculous thing to do. You've got to have faith in your mechanics, in the people who are with you, and you've got to have faith in yourself. When I get into my car I don't think I have ever in my life consciously considered the point of being killed.* If you asked me if it was a dangerous sport, I'd say yes, obviously. But not for me. I would say the only danger to me is if something falls off or somebody spins in front of me where I can't help hitting him, or if I hit oil on the road. But if you asked me didn't I think it dangerous to the point where I might overdrive and go off the road, I'd be insulted. I mean, boy, it's as simple as that.

"It doesn't frighten me to go over the blind brow of a hill at one hundred and sixty or seventy miles an hour. I know I shall make it. I say to myself, if I say anything, that I know how to do this, this is what I have spent my life learning, the chance of anything happening is next to nil, and I'll do it.

"What's the point of living if one's not able to do at least *one* thing?"

*In April 1963 Moss was dining with a girl he had met at Goodwood the night before the accident. Thinking to make him recall and acknowledge this anniversary, she said: "What happened last Easter?" Instantly Moss replied: "I got killed." Then he put down his fork and said: "Whatever made me say that?"

CHAPTER VIII

". . . the faster one goes, the less one cares about
the machinery or the destination."
                                    James Truslow Adams

Chapter VIII

I AM happy that I do not know how many tens of thousands
of words bearing on motor-cars and motor-racing I have
read. The total would, I know, discourage me. It
would seem a monument to futility, for in all that reading
I have not found an adequate and convincing description
of the actual sensation of movement in a racing-car at high
speed, a description that did not demand prior knowledge and understanding. I don't know why this should
be so.

Hemingway and Barnaby Conrad and Kenneth Tynan,
to name three of many, have written clearly about bull-
fighting; Ring Lardner and W. C. Heinz, again among
many, have done as much for boxing; Sir John Hunt and
Sir Edmund Hillary can convey the meaning and the emotion of mountain-climbing, but most descriptions of motor-
racing have been failures.

They do not begin to tell what it means to have behind
one, as Stirling Moss has behind him, a decade and more of
driving, at least 125,000 *miles* of driving as fast as a fast
car can be made to move. No one who has not done this
can express what it means, and not by any means everyone
who *has* done it can tell of it. One hundred and twenty-five
thousand miles—that's five times around the Earth at the
equator—flat out. One must think about it for an instant,
looking down like an astronaut, the globe spinning in space,
and on the rim of it the toy car and the small white figure
in it. When was the last time I drove *five* miles as fast as

the thing I was in would go? When was the last time you did? Five times flat-out around the equator. . . .

"That reminds me, that idea," Stirling Moss said, "of the exhibits one sees sometimes in top-shop windows, a little electric train or a car running on a free-wheeling track, the track spins, the toy's wheels push it away, and the toy stands still. If the earth's speed is a thousand miles an hour at the equator, and I believe that's the figure, then if the whole world had a smooth road around it, and you could get a car up to a thousand miles an hour, would you stand still?"

"I can't think why not," I said. "It's an intriguing idea. To do that would be to reduce speed absolutely to absurdity, wouldn't it? What a thing! A thousand miles an hour— and going nowhere!"

"If you went the other way," Moss said, "*with* the rotation instead of against it, would you do two thousand?"

"Ask Ken Gregory to see about getting the road built," I said. "We'll find out."

"There's the little matter of a car that would do a thousand, too," Stirling said.

"By the time the road's ready, the car will be as well, I daresay," I said. "Think how you'll be denounced in press and pulpit, to coin a phrase. '*Mad Moss motors to nowhere. I did it for kicks, he says.*'"

"That's all I *could* say, and be honest."

"Yes. I'm sure plenty of people have quoted Aldous Huxley to you as saying that speed is the only new sin, the sin of the 20th century, but what he actually did say is that in his view speed provides the only genuinely *modern* pleasure."

"Yes. Certainly it's a great pleasure, speed, and it is modern all right, isn't it? After all sixty miles an hour was

156

first reached within the lifetime of people now living. So it would be hard to quarrel with Huxley over that."

"To what degree *is* it a pleasure, would you say? To start well out, really far out, there used to be an American driver who said that driving so excited him that he often had an erection, and occasionally an orgasm, during a race."

"I think the chap must have been round the bend, don't you?" Stirling said. "A bit abnormal in some fashion or other. I've never had anything like that happen to me, no driver has ever told me of anything of the sort. Mind you, that's not to say it couldn't happen. It probably could. I've heard of that happening to a bullfighter, that kind of excitement."

"A psychologist might think that particular *torero* a bit odd, I'm afraid."

"You mean, of course, because of the connection with death, with killing. Yes. Odd, indeed. But to go back to driving, great speed *is* an intense pleasure, I think it's instinctive and basic. I'm not sure it doesn't run through all mammals, not just humans. You know if you put a dog in a car he'll stick his head out the window into the slipstream and look ahead, and he gives every indication of enjoying the sensations of speed. I know that some dogs do that because the car's exhaust system is leaking, they can pick up the smell though the people in the car cannot, and it distresses them, but that can't always be the reason, and you almost never see a dog with his head *inside* a car if there's a window open. It's true of children, too. A child of two or three will sit up and show signs of pleasure, and so many children's games involve speed, don't they. They don't know where they're going and they don't care."

"That's true."

"One can't really enjoy speed to the absolute limit if there's a destination involved. A destination introduces an element of obligation, makes a job of the whole thing. For real enjoyment, the speed itself must be the purpose. For example, coming out of a corner into a straight, one's purpose is to leave it as fast as possible, and at the other end, one's purpose is to come as close as possible to the corner before doing any braking, and those purposes are in a sense destinations; but in the very middle of the straight, perhaps, one can enjoy the sheer sensation, the sheer delight, of flat-out speed, when you're in top gear, and the pointer on the rev-counter has gone around the dial as far as it *will* go. Oddly, I don't think women have this excitement. I think that when women drive, they always have a destination.

"Probably you're right, Stirling," I said. "Women are more practical. They are less susceptible to aesthetic excitement, one of the reasons women artists, musicians, are rare. But they're not less susceptible to sensual excitement, after all. Haven't you found that the sights and sounds, the drama if you like, of motor-racing, excite some women?"

"Definitely. It may even be true of all women, or nearly all. You will certainly find that a woman is more receptive to an advance during a race, or just before a race, than she is afterward. There's no question about that, and it must be because her level of excitement falls after the race is over.

"In Europe it's quite an accepted thing that when you go motor-racing you take your wife, your girl-friend, mistress, *vahine,* whatever, with you. Most drivers do have a girl and she comes along and decorates the pit. If she can, she takes times. Perhaps she does nothing. With her, the driver can unwind. You come in from dashing around the circuit, it's a fair job, you put a lot into it and then you pull in and you see your girl and it's light relief, it's like reading a mystery novel after being in school all day, and you have a little chat with her while they're changing the tyres or whatever and then you say: 'Well, goodbye, sweetie,' and you're off. And the moment you leave the pits you've forgotten about her, you'd better believe it, you're looking at the rev-counter again.

"There are lots of girls who hang about, of course, as there are around any sport, and of course they're rather different from the regulars, the ones people think of as an essential part of the *equipe*. Even Mercedes, an organization that was very strict with drivers, saw you had enough sleep and so on, they didn't frown on your having a girl-friend. Neubauer might make jokes about them, but he would never make the girl feel she was unwanted. The most he'd do, he might say: 'Now, look here, keep your mind on the job, boy, I'm afraid tonight we've got a meeting and you're not going to go out.' And the strong comradeship drivers generally feel toward each other extends to the girls. Most drivers are easy to get along with anyway, and everyone's nice to the other chap's girl, or girls, as the case may be.

"I won't say *everyone* approves. Alf Francis would approve of the Indianapolis rule: no women in the pits. Obviously I don't agree with him. I think I take my motor-racing pretty seriously, but Alf is *really* in earnest. A man would have to be, to do some of the things he's done. My God, when I think of the times, when we were with H.W.M., when Alf would leave England in a clapped-out Ford transporter with the cars, just enough time, let's say, to get to Monza before a race, drive across France, over the mountains, Italy, non-stop except that he'd probably have to get out and crawl under the van two or three times to put something right, it was forever breaking; get there, unload the cars— and then perhaps have to tear down an engine. There were times when Alf went two straight nights without sleep, and he'd go three, with a few cat-naps. So Alf's entitled to any opinions he has about racing, he's earned the right. But for me, I think a pit's all the better for a bit of crumpet, somebody to wave to, somebody to take your mind off things, if just by chance you come in half a lap ahead, and the transmission in bits.

"And there's the night to think of, after the race. You want to unwind really, no nonsense. Usually the drivers won't be leaving that place directly, there'll be parties, and if it's a city like Brussels, for example, where there are excellent restaurants and some swinging nightclubs, everybody wants to go out. And you may not feel like being alone.

"I used to discipline myself so severely, I would not have intercourse for five days before a race. Later, I began to think, that was going pretty far, who needs to live at all, allowing onself sex two days out of seven? I believed that if I had made love the night before a race, I would be physically just that little bit weaker when I drove, and that belief was enough for me. Then one night before a race at Brands Hatch I was with a girl. We were fond of each other, and I abandoned my rule. Next day I had seven races, quite a few really, only short ones, but seven, and I won the lot! I was really swinging, I was on great form.

"That day didn't altogether change my mind, though. After all, they were short races, I had intervals of rest. The night before a really hard race, Le Mans, Sebring, the *Mille Miglia,* or a G.P. race—no.

"An odd fact, while I don't get a conscious sexual stimulation from driving, as I said, I do get a tremendous stimulation, I think of it as intellectual, that's not the right word, but it's a non-*physical* sensation, and it produces a tranquillity that is very like the tranquillity that follows a deep relationship. Driving does that to me. My mind is calm, but very active, and I feel at peace.

"I know it's been put forward that one drives to prove one's masculinity because it's a masculine sport like bull-fighting and mountain-climbing, things that women really and truly can't do, or never do well. A most *male* thing. I don't know. Anyone who's paid much attention to what some have called the blood sports can name homosexuals who've been boxers, bull-fighters, racing-drivers, but none of the latter, at least, were even close to the first rank. I don't think that I drive to prove I'm a man. I think I drive for a dozen different reasons, but not that one. Still, if it were true, I suppose I'd be the last to know. If there are those who think I drive to prove I'm a man, or that other drivers drive for that reason, fair enough, and good luck to them, they know something that I do not.

"I do think that no woman could become a truly great racing-driver. I didn't see the great women drivers, Elisabetta Juneck, Kay Petre, 'Bill' Wisdom, Gwenda Stewart and the others, but I understand that only Juneck could worry top men drivers in *grand prix* cars, and she didn't drive for long. I don't believe that lack of physical strength, ability to hold the car, that sort of thing, keeps women from driving as well as men. My sister Pat, for example, certainly has ample physical energy to do three hundred miles flat-out in a *grand prix* car. I doubt Pat would even have to go into her reserve. It isn't lack of strength. It's just that women are almost never *personally* competitive. In rallying, which is a less demanding form of racing, there are women who are very good indeed, there are women who will beat all but the top men, and beat them easily. But rallying is running against the clock, and women do that sort of thing very well. Also rallying makes much of minute detail, and women are good at that, too. For instance, everywhere in the world where very small machines are being assembled, tiny radios, sub-miniature ball-bearings and that sort of thing, you'll find women are doing the work because men can't do it as well. Anything involving patience, detail. But women will not compete, as the Spanish say, *mano-a-mano,* hand-to-hand. They will not go into really brutal competition with another person; they will not, or they cannot, as a rule, reach the highest plane of the competitive urge, where a man will say: 'Right, now I've had enough of hanging about, now I'll have a go, now we're going to separate the men from the boys here.' No, they won't do that. Mind, I'm not saying that's wrong, or a bad thing, I'm just saying that's the way it is. When someone says that if women ran the governments of the world there'd be no wars, no argument comes from *my* corner of the room. It's probably true.

"You'll notice that in driving a woman passenger, sometimes she'll pay attention to how fast you're going, she'll watch the speedometer, and when you go over the limit at which she's comfortable, you'll sense that she's pushing her right foot on the floor-board, or she'll reach for the grab-handle, and then of course, unless you're a hopeless clot, you'll back off ten miles an hour. But if the speedometer is disconnected, or unlighted at night, she may not object at all, providing you work up speed slowly and drive very smoothly. In other words, she's probably just not aware.

"I had a date with a girl one time, we were in a Mini-Cooper, I've forgotten where we were going, but it was a bit of a journey, and after fifty or sixty miles she told me she thought it was very amusing, that a friend of hers who had an M.G.A., a solicitor or something, drove much faster than I did. I asked her what was the fastest she thought we'd been doing, the speedo cable was broken, she couldn't tell from that, and she said, oh, around fifty, which was pretty funny because she was about thirty miles an hour out of the way. Of course, she was no doubt a poor judge of speed, but she didn't think she'd been going fast because she hadn't felt any violent movements of any kind, and that's how most people judge. I should say right here, however, that I can think of six non-professionals who, in my opinion, drive really well—and four of them are women.

"Another woman—let's say a top woman driver—will sit there, you can go very fast indeed, right on up, and she'll be tranquil, outwardly at least, and she may say she's enjoying the ride, but I believe that what she's enjoying are the points of technique she finds interesting, she's not enjoying speed for the sake of speed. Fair enough, most passengers do not, but I at least have never found a woman who I think enjoyed speed for its own sake, either driving or being driven. I think it's a peculiarly male reaction. It satisfies something fundamental in men. You and I can certainly expect to live to see trains doing 150 and 200 miles an hour, and people will be mad to travel on them, you'll see. As for aircraft, the *Concorde,* the jet passenger plane the British and French governments are planning, will do about 1,450 miles an hour!"

"Yes," I said, "but you can't have windows in anything that's doing 1,450 miles an hour, the passengers will be sitting there reading or watching a cinema, perhaps the captain will come on the blower and say there's a tail-wind and the aeroplane is indicating 1,600, they'll think: 'My, that's quick, isn't it?'—and go back to watching the screen, they won't have any sensation of speed at all."

"True enough," Stirling said. "When you get down to it, speed matters only in a motor-car or on a motor-bike.

Nothing else goes fast enough, on land, carrying only one man, or at the most, two; speed on water seems to me to be imprecise, uncontrolled; speed under-water, or in the air, doesn't produce any sensation, really, doesn't count.

"No. For me it has to be in a motor-car, in contact with the earth, if not by much, and a man using his hands, his feet, his eyes, his brain to balance inertia and momentum and gravity and centrifugal force in an equation that changes ten times a second; in a vehicle, if you like, that represents the best efforts of the most skilful specialist designers in the world, and a beautiful thing, too—you must admit, there have been very few ugly racing-cars; *that* is living, and in the company, if you like, of the dozen or fifteen men in the world who can do what you're doing, and, let's say, on a real circuit like the Nurburg Ring, *that* is motor-racing, and when you think of it in that fashion, as it really is, you realize that it's absurd to compare it with any other sport. I'm not being provincial, I am not narrow-minded, I hope I'm not, but I really do believe that: there is nothing in life so satisfying. Caracciola said it years ago, that it was the most intoxicating sensation in life, something like that. And it is!"

"Hear, hear!" I said. "And hot sunshine and a bright blue sky!"

"Blue sky, nothing!" Stirling said. "In the pouring rain, in a half-cloudburst. The sun coming out in the last lap, if you like, for the finish."

I looked down the long settee at him, immaculate in hand-sewn Italian loafers, grey flannel slacks, a blue jacket; he was silent for ten seconds; he was waiting for me to say something, looking at me; this was long after Goodwood, after the Atkinson Morley Hospital, but before his second trip back to St. Thomas's, where they would saw a piece of bone out of his pelvis and prop up his left eye-socket with it; now his left eye was lower in his face than the right, and the eye itself pointed off at a slight angle, looking past me. 'You are a damned strange man,' I thought, 'and there is certainly a hell of a hot little fire burning in you somewhere. I don't know where you're headed; I hope you get there. But you won't be going motor-racing any more.'

I walked over to the big window and looked out. There are temporary buildings in the street, the view is not enchanting. Life looks real out there, though, and sometimes, in contrast, the living room in the Moss house seems unreal in its newness and its shiny near-perfection, in the eerie sensation that there are many motors humming unseen, hidden in the walls.

I came back.

"The transport pilots say flying is no fun any more," I said, "because the black box does everything and if you want to land in London you have to start letting down over Paris. There aren't many generations of pilots left. Of fighter pilots, none, we're watching the last one. Can you think of Formula cars without drivers, big black boxes doing the steering and the shifting, and treading on the loud-pedal?"

"No, never," Stirling said. "The race would be totally without excitement."

"Do you think that means that people come to see races in the hope of seeing the drivers hurt?"

"No, but I don't think we'll see that question answered definitely until someone works out a way to fit 50,000 lie-detectors to 50,000 people watching a *grand prix* race. But driverless cars, never. That would ruin everything."

"What, then, in the year 2000?"

"Smaller cars, lighter, lower. This will be possible because you'll have a smaller engine: a gas-turbine, perhaps, or a Wankel engine about as big as your head, perhaps even a steam engine, maybe a tiny 16-cylinder petrol engine with cylinders the size of florins. The car will have 250 miles an hour available, and I'm probably being conservative. The suspension and the adhesion will be fantastic, incredible, the car will track through any corner, the drift will be forgotten, and the words understeer and oversteer will be quaint historical terms that nobody uses any more."

"The driver?"

"I think he'll lie down flat, his face right up in front next to the accident, he'll steer with a tiller or with levers, have a brake-pedal for his left foot and a throttle for his right. He'll have a periscope rear-view mirror. The transmission, if there is one, will be automatic, of course. No gear-shifting whatever."

"Won't it be rough to drive in that position, Stirling?"

"They said it would be rough to drive a Formula One car with the seats turned practically into hammocks, but we did it. And those cars are comfortable once one's in them, you know, very comfortable."

"Yes. And they said the old pre-World War II Auto-Unions couldn't be handled, with the driver way up in front."

"Right," Stirling said. "But they managed, up to around 200 miles an hour. Rosemeyer. Nuvolari. It was only a matter of getting used to the position. I had a Kieft years ago; I sat so far forward in it that if I crept up on the grid I'd reach out and wind it back with the front wheels! I never thought that car dicey in the least."

"All right, but with your face *ahead* of the front wheels, and about six inches off the deck!"

"Ken, did you ever stop to think, when the man runs a Boeing or a Comet jet down the runway at 160 miles an hour, that's where he is, out in front, he's sitting so far in front of his wheels it's not to be believed. It would just be a matter of getting used to it, driving up front lying down, just a matter of conditioning, like everything else. Perhaps you'd do what the Auto-Union people did, recruit motor-bike riders, men who'd never driven a racing-car, and so had nothing to unlearn, they thought that was the normal place to be up in front. Rosemeyer was the best Auto-Union driver, and he was a bike-rider."

"Would you like to drive a car like that, Stirling, a 250-mile-an-hour *grand prix* car, lying flat on your belly?"

"Now, yes. In the year 2000, no. Do you realize that in the year 2000 I'll be over 45 years old?"

"No! It can't be true!"

"It is, though. I'll be getting on!"

"So will I. Very depressing notion. Let's drop it. Let's talk about something else. Girls, for instance."

"That reminds me," Stirling said, "I want to tell you about . . . turn the thing off, you're closer to it, pull the plug, you've nearly finished that reel anyway. . . ."

CHAPTER IX

"You may give him good advice, but who can
give him the wit to take it?"

Thomas Fuller

CHAPTER IX

"Young people write to me all the time," Stirling said, "asking me how to get to be a racing-driver. I'm not sure I know the honest answer."

"I get letters like that now and then," I said, "asking me how to be a writer. The honest answer is that if you have to ask, you will never be a writer, you may be a reporter, or something like that, but you'll never be a writer, and I should think it's true about being a race-driver, too. At least about coming to be what you call a real driver, a pro. You know what Louis Armstrong, wasn't it, said when someone asked him something about jazz: 'You got to *ask*, man, you ain't never gonna find out!'"

"Yes. That's right. People on the outside don't understand the heart of the matter; you'll notice they put too much emphasis on the *instrument,* on equipment, on mechanical things. You hear people in sports cars, or in Minis, now, blasting along and shifting down for red lights and all that. It would be hard to explain to them, I suppose, that a racing-driver doesn't care which way the gears work, really, or what gear he's in. You just know that if you shove the thing forward and away from you to the right you'll go up, and straight back, you'll go up, and back and toward you you'll go down. You don't have to wait for valve-bounce to know it's time to change gears; you just know the thing has come to a point where it can't put out any more power in the gear it's in so you go looking for another one—but quickly, quickly.

"I have *no* idea, with any car I've driven, what speed is represented by 7,200 revs. I have *no* idea. I don't care, either. Speed is purely relative in racing. A hundred seems fast until you've done it, then 150 seems fast—until you've done 200. What does count in speed, is sensing how much of it you can use. If you go into a hundred-mile-an-hour corner at 101, that's too fast, and 99 is too slow—and you'd better be able to feel the difference in the seat of your pants.

"I like to teach people to drive. When I lost my licence and couldn't drive for a year, I taught Valerie Pirie to drive, actually re-taught her, and I would say I did a good job, wouldn't you, you've ridden with her."

"Yes. I'm a bad passenger, but I like riding with Valerie. She drove me across town to St. Thomas's one day during the big fog, she went as quickly as she always does but it was a nice secure ride."

"Of course people don't understand that there's practically no connection between driving on the road and driving on a circuit, driving to go somewhere, and driving in competition. I have taken various people around circuits. Some are frightened, but many more are exhilarated. As a matter of principle I always go slowly because I don't *want* them to be frightened, and I certainly don't want to expose them to unnecessary hazard. Say if the car will do 160 down the straight then I'll do something around 130 or 140, depending on my judgement of the individual. They don't know what's happening. They think they're flying. It would be very hard to make them understand that at, say, 120 on a straight on a Formula One car, a professional feels—rightly or wrongly—that there's nothing that can possibly happen that he can't manage with ease, unless it's two wheels coming off or something of that sort.

"I maintain that a good driver can take a person out and drive very fast and the other person won't know what's going on. No jolt, no jerk, no swing, no oversteer and that sort of thing. If you build speed slowly, you will spoil most persons' judgement on that factor."

"You know in the early days of racing," I told Stirling, "before World War I, say, now and again a riding mechanic, they often didn't know how to drive at all, would be hurt, because after a few long laps in the eighties and nineties, the car would come into the pits at thirty and the man would just step off, thinking it was going at a walking pace."

"It seems to me that mechanics were always getting run over in the old days," Stirling said. "So many things surprised them. Of course, they were pioneering, weren't they, finding out. One of the essentials of racing is to know when you're going to have an accident and know early and accept it. That's terribly important, and it takes a lot of schooling, a lot of self-discipline, to come to it. Most people, in emergency, go through a panic-reaction, they think: 'A terrible thing is going to happen to me I wish it weren't going to happen to me I hope it doesn't happen to me.' That sort of thing. What they *should* be thinking is: 'The lift is falling. What can I do in the next two seconds to save myself?' If you've spent four or five years training yourself for that moment, you might have a chance, you might be able to see, identify and hit the emergency-stop button, or failing that you might be able to watch the shaft and just before the bottom, jump up so as to be off the floor when it hits, I wonder if that would work, I suppose not; or you might have time to throw yourself down on the floor and spread the shock over all of your body instead of taking the lot straight up your legs. But if you just stand there with your brain in neutral, so to speak, you'll be hurt.

"It's like going into a corner and making a mess of it; you must know early on and accept it and don't fight it. If one goes into a corner in an oversteer slide, it doesn't matter, you or I can set up a slide and get out of it at will, but if we go into a corner normally, and hit oil and *then* it starts to slide, maybe it's less of a slide than we could incite at will, but we're lagging *behind* the slide in the sense that our reactions are behind and so it becomes very much more important. You must be able to balance and unbalance the car at will, whenever you want to do it. If you hit oil unexpectedly you may need both hands and your legs and your teeth to get out of it. I say 'unexpectedly'. Oil on the circuit is one of the worst things, one of the frightening things, but I can remember times I've gone looking for oil patches and run over every one I could see, when I was down to the fabric on my tyres, and had no chance to stop for new ones: oil is easier on tyres than concrete. You watch for oil all the time, you see it as a slick a long way ahead, and that's all right. The nightmare thing is to come around a corner going hard, and find that someone's dropped a couple of quarts in the middle of it. You're going to be busy, then.

"One must know oneself, to do anything at all in any kind of work. It's so easy for a man to be deceived about the one person he should know best: himself. For instance, novice drivers get hurt because they're going into a corner at what they reckon to be a pretty good rate, and what is in fact, for them, a pretty good rate, and someone runs by them in a similar car. So they think: 'I must have misjudged this bend, it must be a faster one than I'd thought, because there goes old what's-his-face, he's been around longer than I have, he must know.' So, next time around, they take it faster—and go into the bushes. No *corner* is faster or slower. Individual men are faster or slower. Indi-

vidual cars are faster or slower. You must know what your
limit is. And if it changes, you must know what it is each
day.

"Drivers who have on days and off days most likely are
hurt or killed on an off day. The worst thing you can do
in racing is to drive beyond the line of your capabilities on
a given day. Just because you've done three minutes forty
seconds at such-and-such a circuit on one day doesn't mean
you should do it tomorrow or the day afterward. To know
you can do it, yes; to strive to do it, yes; but to accept nothing
less—that is foolishness.

"A driver who is not on form *every* time he gets into the
car, and who doesn't understand this, and will not or cannot
accept it—he's asking for trouble.

"I can't remember having an off day and knowing it.
[Denis Jenkinson says that Moss never did have an off day.]
That doesn't mean that it didn't happen. But I can't remember its happening. I must have had off days, although I
probably had *fewer* than most drivers because I tried very
hard indeed to maintain a level: a level of physical fitness,
of mental tranquillity, of detail, of readiness, and so on and
on. But I must have had off days, and the fact I'm alive
now most likely means that I knew it at the time and
accepted it. Or else that I was just terribly lucky and got
away with it.

"I would try to bring myself to a peak at the right time
for a peak. In practice as a matter of principle I used to
learn the circuit and then do one or two laps and then go
in and get the car set up properly, you know, tyre-pressures,
shock-absorber settings, roll-bar adjustments, gear-ratios, all
those things that one must do to get an individual car down
to micrometer fitness for a given circuit. Then I'd do another
lap or two, but I wouldn't attempt a really fast lap until

the very end of the practice period. My idea, of course—
and everybody else's—was to cross the finish line just as the
practice closed, so that if I had made the fastest time, which
I always tried to do, it would stand, no one could go out and
beat it, and I would have the inside position on the grid next
day, for the race proper. I remember one day early on, I
was in a hurry, I wanted to go out and try for a fast one,
and Alf Francis said: 'Why don't you wait, let the sun go
down a little, you'll feel better, it will be cool, the car will
run better.' So I waited, and I thought about it, and I
probably brought myself up to a peak. I don't remember if
I had the fastest time that day, but I remember that it was
very quick.

"Racing is a business, after all, as well as all the other
things it is. Although sometimes I wonder if it's a business
for John Cooper. Unlike almost every other important
racing-car constructor in the world, Cooper makes no
passenger cars, which is the profitable end of the trade. All
right, B.R.M. doesn't, but B.R.M. is a subsidiary of another
company, and A. J. Watson doesn't, in the States, but he has
practically a one-man firm, I understand, making a few
Indianapolis cars a year. But I think that considering the
long hours Cooper puts in, he could most likely make rather
more money doing something else. So, plainly, he must very
much like motor-racing, and I think he's to be admired for
that attitude."

"Is it because motor-racing is a business, Stirling," I said,
"that the Grand Prix Drivers' Association was set up? Is
the G.P.D.A. a kind of trade union?"

"It is not!" he said. "The G.P.D.A. was formed for the
general betterment of motor-racing. I'm president at the
moment, so I think I can say with authority that it is no part
of a trade union. I think that idea would finish racing off

in a big hurry. I mean that there's nothing militant about the G.P.D.A.; we would never go on strike, that sort of thing. What we try to do, we try to induce promoters to improve the circuits, make then safer, mainly for the spectator. We do *not* advocate taking out trees, for instance, eliminating things that make for interest. We don't want 'spin-off' zones and that sort of thing. We do like circuits like Laguna Seca in California, which is a difficult circuit, a dangerous circuit, it's definitely not a club circuit, but we like it. We like the natural hazards. We'd like to race around Hyde Park or Central Park without any changes at all in the topography. We accept the hazards, as at Monaco, of hitting a building or going over a drop; after all, it's no fun gambling for match-sticks.

"The G.P.D.A. would like to have a membership in the F.I.A., the Féderation Internationale de l'Automobile, to represent the drivers. Everybody else is represented, on the F.I.A., the world governing body of the sport, everybody but the people who do, after all, provide the primary ingredient in the sport—the racing. Even if the F.I.A. wouldn't grant us a voting membership, we'd like at least to be on hand so that when things like the absurdly high windshield of a few years back was made mandatory for sports cars, we could argue about it. As it was, we had to sit there for twelve, fifteen hours, at Le Mans, trying to look *over* the thing, but you certainly couldn't look *through* it, covered with oil, rubber, dust and mosquitoes as it very quickly was. At the moment, the F.I.A. are being much more helpful to us than in the past.

"Jo Bonnier went to the meeting in Paris on our behalf late in 1962 to talk about the new cars, and the F.I.A. people were staggered to know that we think the low, light Formula One cars comfortable. They are, you know. The F.I.A.

thought those old crates we used to drive, those things you
sat in bolt upright, were comfortable and, in fact, they were
lousy.

"That's not to say that the present Formula One, or
grand prix cars are perfect, they certainly are not. The
constructors are building the cars too small. We met with
B.R.M. and Cooper and Lotus and we tried to draw up
what we felt were standards for reasonable cockpit dimen-
sions. The cars are comfortable, yes, but they fit very tightly
around one. On the late 1962 Porsche, the steering wheel
had to be detachable in the old-fashioned way to let the
driver get in, and even then it was hard for a big man like
Gurney. On the Lotus 25, you have to shift gears by bending
your wrist back and forth. There's no room for moving
your arm. That's bloody ridiculous.

"I think most of us in the G.P.D.A. are against seat-belts
in G.P. cars. I like seat-belts in closed cars, but in a racing-
car I want to be thrown out, or have the choice, mainly
because of the danger of fire. I once bailed out of an E.R.A.
when it went afire. I slowed it in a ditch and jumped; had
I been wearing a belt I shouldn't have had time to undo the
thing. I will not use a belt in a race. At a race in Riverside,
U.S.A., I was told that seat-belts were mandatory. It was
going to cost me thousands of dollars, but I told the mechanics to load the car and pack up. The promoters came
around, and we compromised. I said they could put a seat-
belt in the car, if they liked, so long as the ends were buckled
together under the seat, so they couldn't fly around, and
so that no one could think, looking into the car, that I was
going to use it. The thing was put right out of sight. But
it was in the car and I suppose that satisfied the insurance
brokers or whatever. I thought it was a piece of flaming
hypocrisy.

"The constructors, the car manufacturers?—Except for Mercedes-Benz, which is after all a huge corporation, and is really a first-cabin operation in every way, and Enzo Ferrari, who has such a tremendous backlog of experience and must be himself at least on the border-line of genius, most constructors are small operators, on a tight budget, and one must make allowances sometimes. They are after all mostly business men, with the business man's problems and outlook.

"In mechanics you find a very high degree of ethics, much higher, I can tell you, than you'll find in some other, and distinctly more prosperous categories in racing. The mechanics work terribly hard, they aren't paid much, they certainly aren't getting rich. They're a bit like nurses. I remember that when I persuaded John Heath to give the mechanics ten per cent of the prize money, early in the 1950's, that was considered a pretty radical idea. A mechanic can lose a race for you with a twist of his wrist in the middle of the night, and when did you ever hear of its being done, except in the cinema? In a decade and a half of racing, I *never* heard of its being done. Alf Francis and I used to have some terrible quarrels, just this side of physical violence, some of them, but his calling me everything he could think of never left me anything but perfectly willing to put my life in his hands.

"I'd get furious with Alf over something that had gone wrong with the car, and I'd say: 'The trouble with you, Alf, you can't drive, you haven't got the guts to go out in the car and see what happens to it out there.' And he'd say: 'You're a coward, Stirling, you may make yourself do it, but you're a coward'—forgetting that the classic definition of a brave man is a coward who'll go and do it anyway. And a couple of times, Alf, being no coward himself, got into the car and went out and stuck his foot into it a little way and came back white and shaking, so that he had to take a couple of deep breaths before he could climb out of the thing.

"Alf reminds me of the story about the man everyone hated, he was a hopeless clot and stole from widows and orphans and all that; finally he died, and people who knew him were standing around at the funeral and no one could think of anything good to say about this bloke. And one man spoke up and said: 'I remember, when we were in school, he was a very good speller.' The man who spoke up would be Alf. If he thinks you're a clot, he'll say so, and to anybody who asks him, but if he once saw you pick up a stray cat, he'll put that in as well. He's even honest enough to admit he can't drive, and that's as honest as you can get!

"Only two men have ever admitted to me that they weren't expert drivers. One was Gilbert Harding, the great television personality, he isn't living now, and the other one I can't remember.

"There are two things no man will admit he can't do well, apparently: drive and make love. And I imagine that's significant in some fashion. A man will admit anything else, that he can't dance, he can't ski-jump, he can't play the zither. But in a pretty wide acquaintance, and all over the world this side of the Iron Curtain, I've met two men who said: 'Right, I'm not a good driver.' And you can imagine how many men, out of that same acquaintance, have admitted they weren't great lovers. Not two, boy. And not one. Not one!"

CHAPTER X

"Non possunt primi esse omnes in omni
tempore."

Laberius

CHAPTER X

O NE dark afternoon in December, 1962, during the worst fog London had had for fifteen years, I went around to St. Thomas's Hospital to see Stirling, recuperating from one of the operations meant to correct the injuries of the Easter crash. He was wearing the beginnings of a beard; a gauze bandage had been spiralled around his head like a turban. He was surrounded by the standard Moss-in-hospital accoutrements: a stack of mail, a dictating machine, tape recorder, radio, flowers and fruit, a pretty nurse. The supervisor came looking for the nurse, and we were alone.

"I came in here on instruments," I said. "I wouldn't want to say it's foggy, lest you construe it as an insult to your native land. You might use your massive influence to have the Home Office cancel my residence permit. Still, there *has* been a little low-lying mist out there for the last couple of days. I could hardly find the street, never mind the hospital."

"You see? I picked a good time to be here," he said. "Have some tea. There are chocolates in that box. Have some. You won't get chocolates like that in America, boy."

"Rule, Britannia," I said. The chocolates were excellent. Dutch.

"That sister who was here," Moss said, "when you came barging in and broke up the party, she was telling me she'd never seen a motor-race."

"You'll fix that, I imagine, as soon as they turn you loose?"

"I just might," he said. [When he was released, Moss took his nurses to the theatre *en masse*.] "But what I am trying to get to, if you'll leave off interrupting me, was that she said being married to a racing driver must be like being married to a soldier. What do you think about that notion?"

"I think she was making a nice try," I said. "She's pretty, too."

"Have some more tea. I was thinking a little bit about that. I was thinking about how it must have been when Katie and I were married, and she was watching me race all the time. It couldn't have been too jolly, that continuous pressure of knowing that someone she was rather fond of was out there risking his neck. She hadn't got as much faith in me, I presume, as I had. I never reckoned I was risking my neck, but I'm sure she must have done."

I looked at him. I wasn't sure he was serious, but he was.

"Do you know what you're saying?" I said. "Here you are, flat in bed, back in hospital yet another time, full of miscellaneous holes and bone-grafts and best surgeons' hemstitching, and you say you weren't risking your neck! What are you doing here, then?"

"Yes—but I *shouldn't* be here!" Stirling said. "It surprised me. It more than surprised me, I just can't believe it still. I just can't understand it. Did I make a mistake? Fair enough, I make mistakes all the time. I make mistakes in addition. I paint a room the wrong colour. Okay. But not when my life's at stake."

"Oh, I don't know about that," I said. "You admit you've driven a lot of very fragile motor-cars, cars you knew were likely to break."

"That's true," Stirling said. "When it comes to choosing a car, I think of safety very little. If I were driving for a manufacturer who built a car I thought was unsafe, I don't think I'd have much to say as to whether I'd drive it; if it was *too* bad I'd leave, but it would have to be very bad indeed before I would.

"I've driven most kind of cars, Formula Three 500's, touring cars, sports cars, sprints, *grand prix,* landspeed cars— and to me a car is individual, yes, but still it's the same as the next car, too. If the thing's got four wheels and will move forward and backward and it's got so many gears, right, I'll get in, and I'll go, if there's a steering wheel and a clutch, fair enough, and a mechanic I trust will tell me he has no reason to believe anything is actually just on the point of falling off it. Basically the only thing I care about is: can the car be *balanced?* Or, as you say in the States, will it *handle?*

"Racing is rather like painting to me: the car is only the instrument, as paints are to a painter. All right, one car is better than another, fine, and one kind of paint is better than another, very well, but it really doesn't matter, the painter creates with whatever he has at hand, and if he hasn't anything better he'll use a child's set of crayons. Give Picasso a broken two-shilling set of crayons and he'll give you something worth two thousand pounds. After all, I think driving is an art. I really do maintain that.

"My attitude toward cars is unusual, I realize that. Most people specialize and in many cases I think they're wise to do so. There are drivers today, say Brabham if you like, who might be foolish to try to race touring cars and sports cars. He's probably broadening out now, but certainly there was a time when he would have been unwise to do it—and you'll notice that he did not.

"Fangio did not, either. He drove *grand prix* cars almost
entirely, after 1949. Even sports cars he drove only reluctantly. Maybe he and Jack were both wiser than I, concen-
trating on what they did best."

"But you don't know what you did best," I said. "And
neither does anyone else, at least as among *grand prix,* sports
car races, and rallies."

"There's that," he said, "and then there's the other thing:
you're *meant* to do what you can do. If a musician can
compose *and* conduct *and* play an instrument, he should.
If a writer can write novels *and* plays, he should. You owe
that to yourself."

"*Grand prix* driving carries the biggest rewards."

"That's not a reason. I'm as greedy as the next man, but
that's not enough reason. A professional is a driver who races
out of pride. He wants to win because he wants to beat you,
not just to get the extra few dollars or pounds or francs, or
whatever. I don't know anyone racing today, or who was
racing in 1960, 1961, 1962, purely for money. One would
like to get first place rather than second place because there's
a bit more money in it, right, and that's fair enough, but
that's not what really pushes the professional on. The real
pro will try just as hard for no money, or little money, as
for a lot. I remember two days of racing at Roskilde in
Denmark, various events all counting together in the end.
I won, and I was handed about £30. I was happy about
winning. I gave the money to the mechanics and told them
to go out and have a ball.

"It's the amateur who has, in my view, what is commonly
held to be the 'pro' attitude. It's the amateur who wants the
material things: the silver cup for his mantelpiece and so
on. And it's the bloody amateur who'll come around afterward, after you've given him a thorough clobbering, and

say: 'All right, you did win, but then, you have the right
axle ratio; you have the right tyres and I didn't; after all,
you've done many more races on this circuit than I have.'
[On an Australian circuit Moss made fastest time of the day
in a Lotus, was told: "After all, it's a Lotus circuit". He
got into a Cooper and broke his own mark.] Among pro-
fessionals you *never* hear an excuse. A professional will *never*
come up to you and complain, afterward."

"True. When I said there were greater rewards in *grand
prix* driving, than in other kinds, I meant not only money,
I meant the championship of the world."

"I know you did. People ask: 'Aren't you upset about
not being world champion? Doesn't it bother you, that you
were runner-up five times?' And the answer is, in honesty,
that the first year I was pretty much upset, it would be correct to say, very much upset. But the disappointment got
less each time. Partially it was just conditioning, a second
disappointment is easier to bear than the first, a third is
easier than the second. Partially it was something else, even
now I'm not sure what it was, but I might say it was the
realization that while having the championship would mean
perhaps a lot to Stirling Moss Limited, it might not mean
much to Stirling Moss. Do you understand?"

"Yes."

"Very well. Assume I am *not* flat on my back with a
couple of drainage-tubes stuck in me. Assume I'm in a
motor car, and in one of those races like Morocco in 1958,
one of those the championship hung on. Assume I've got
half a lap on the second-place man. The car is going like
a ruddy bomb, I can have 9,000 revs. any time I want to
put my foot on it, the gear-box could pull a train, I've got
petrol, oil and rubber to burn and throw away. Unless I
run off the course, no one can catch me, and if I win, I'm

champion. Do you know what I'd do, today? I'd pull in, I'd shut the thing off, I'd sit on the pit-counter and have a cup of tea and watch the rest of the race. And you know I mean it, and you know I'd do it. Why?

"Because I'd rather go down in history as the man who never won the championship than as the man who won it once. If I won it once, what of that? Mike Hawthorn won it once. If one wins it twice, does that mean one is a better driver than Mike? I think Mike Hawthorn was a splendid person, he did a lot for motor-racing, I liked him, and I very much indeed wish he were still with us. But I didn't consider him very consistent as a driver. When he had an 'on' day he was very, very good. If he liked a circuit, as he liked Rheims—Mike really did feel that Rheims was his personal property—right, he'd beat Fangio himself on it. If he didn't like a race, and he didn't like the tough ones, the Mille Miglia, the Targa Florio, Sebring, he wasn't mad keen about the Nurburg Ring either, he'd either not run in it or he'd stroke it. I had more respect for Mike as a man than as a driver."

I interrupted Stirling.

"You said that Alf Francis had earned a right to his opinions about motor-racing," I said. "Haven't you? I knew Mike Hawthorn slightly, and I know you well, and anyone who thinks you were ever remotely jealous of anything Mike Hawthorn could do in an automobile is out of his mind.

"I think that you did envy Mike his ability to laugh at life now and again, to say that he didn't give a damn, and mean it. Mike could do some things that you absolutely could not do. For instance, you absolutely could not have gone into Louise and Peter Collins's bathroom, run a tub, and got into it with all your clothes on. You'd have thought that mad. And you'd have been right, because it *was* a mad thing to do. And I daresay, a few hours later, Mike might have wished he hadn't done it, just as you might wish you could get out of yourself, get out of the character of Stirling Moss long enough to *have* done it. Do I have a corner of the truth there somewhere?"

Moss said: "Yes. But now I feel freer in myself. I could do it now, if I felt like doing it. But somehow there seem other things to get on with."

"Right. And it has not a damned thing to do with racing, with the automobile. And you *must* say what you think. You are expected to. You have no right not to. If some clots jump on you for saying what you think, that's too bad. With the first shilling you take from the public, you throw away your right to complain about public criticism. That's just the way things are. When Harry Truman was President of the United States, and people complained to him about public pressures on them, he would say: 'If you can't stand the heat, get out of the kitchen.' As for not criticising people because they're dead, that's juvenile nonsense. Who'd write history, if that were the rule?"

"All right," Stirling said. "So Mike won the championship once, and Phil Hill won it once, and Graham won it once, and Jack Brabham won it twice. Do I have to win it three times to prove I'm a better driver than Jack is? Fangio won it five times. If I won it six times, would that make me a better driver than Fangio? No, it wouldn't. Winning it six times won't make me *as* good a driver as Juan Manuel Fangio, and winning it ten times wouldn't make me a better driver, because I am not. Fangio was better than I was, and that's that.

"One day I was saying to a friend that I didn't know, really, when the championship had lost meaning for me.

Katie was with us, and she said, 'I know when it was, it was in 1958.' I thought about that for a long time and I realized that she was right. I tried for it just as hard, in 1959, 1960, 1961, but that was when the meaning went out of it for me. Five years ago, 1958."

CHAPTER XI

"The secret of life is in art."
Oscar Wilde

What is art, and who is an artist? Millions of us, watching *That Was The Week That Was,* have laughed to see Timothy Birdsall, before an easel, miming, with searing self-confidence, a 'pop' artist who explains that his *collage* of crude lines, gross colours and tacked-on fish-paste tins is authentic art. But those who scorn abstract art, non-representational, non-objective art, everything we call 'modern', are no more valuable to society than the fraudulent artist. They are ignorant where he is venal.

To explain his work to a bright child, an abstract artist might say: "Composers used to make music that sounded like birds singing, or the wind, or waves on the sea-shore. They don't do this any more, they put notes together to make a pleasant sound. I put colours together to make a pleasant sight. Also, sometimes, when I look at a rose, it reminds me of a baby with its mouth open. Sometimes I paint the rose. Sometimes I paint the baby. Sometimes I paint both."

An American woman writing in *The Atlantic Monthly* magazine said, as many have before her, that it was the ability to paint the rose as a rose that gave license to paint it as a baby's mouth. An old truth, but she had a new idea: let every abstract painter exhibit, with his non-representational work, a classic nude, a landscape and a still-life. This would eliminate the frauds. It would not bother the others. Picasso may see a third eye in his wife's forehead today, but half a century ago he did a full-length male nude in nearly photographic fidelity. He has chosen to work in his present style. It has not chosen him. We must face the fact that Picasso, 300 years from now, may be considered classic and conservative, as Rembrandt, 300 years ago, was considered irresponsible and radical.

Art, then, may be a blue-faced horse with one square eye. If art, in the dictionary definition, is "a subject in which high skill may be exercised in an effort to state truth or create beauty," then the witless juggler of Notre Dame was an artist, though he was hopelessly unfitted to sharpen a pencil for such as Leonardo da Vinci.

"To state truth or create beauty." When Katherine Mansfield wrote the line: "A cold wind ran down the street like a thin dog," she was stating a truth in a memorable and beautiful fashion. If she had never written another line, and if that one line had been read by only one person, it would have attested her artistry.

Bad art floods the world. Stages from Moscow to Tokyo, the long way, sag under the weight of cynical, fraudulent drama; critics have a new name for a certain kind of literary work: a 'non-book'. Shallow, silly poetry, photography that is pompous and pretentious, architecture that relates to Corbusier and Saarinen only as money relates to the bank from which it was stolen, such stuff surrounds us. In such a milieu, the fleeting sight of a genuine evocation of beauty, like Katherine Mansfield's eleven words, or a glittering, imperious stare by Sir Laurence Olivier, have the value of that which is rare as well as precious.

Katherine Mansfield's eleven words, if they were all she ever wrote, would be as truly art as any eleven words of Shakespeare's among his tens of thousands of words. Artists, like other people, come both great and small, and have short

194

lives or long. And art lives for a moment, or nearly forever.
He's a fool who would judge between an *entrechat* of
Nijinsky and the pillars of the Parthenon.

When Stirling Moss suggested to me, several years ago,
that some few men, in some few moments of driving,
achieved an art form, I thought the proposition untenable.
I know better now. It is not untenable. It is perfectly valid.
To see a driver of the first rank, running at night in the
rain at Le Mans, let us say, a rooster-tail of spray behind,
committing himself to the bend just past the pits, laying out,
as he runs up to it at 150 miles an hour, the placement of the
parabolic curve, its profile rigidly prescribed by the laws of
physics, that will take him threading through the bend, and
around three slower cars in it, to see this is to see a truth
stated, and in beauty. You will not see such a thing often.
You may watch many races and never see it, or anything
like it, but when you do see it you will remember it, so that
even years later, awake in the night, hearing someone run
an engine too fast, a street away, the high howl of it, passing
the very note, will re-light the scene at Le Mans on the
screen of your mind. The idea that driving can be art seems
strange only because so few people have seen it close and
clearly and because the instrument of its creation, the motor-
car, seems a crude device for such a purpose. But the device,
the instrument, the means—these are not important.

In Tokyo there lives a man named Masutatsu Oyama, a
Korean. Oyama is a big man. His face is flat and bland,
and seems on the point of a smile. Oyama is fluent in
Korean and Japanese but when he speaks in English it is
usually only to say: "Thank you" or "You are very kind".
He is usually silent. He tends to sit quietly, his hands resting
on his thighs; people around him fall silent; an aura of pure
calm, peace, soaring, unreachable serenity surrounds the

man, and one begins to think, after a few minutes, that one should be able to photograph it, for it seems as real, at least, as smoke.

Is Masutatsu Oyama a philosopher, or a priest? No. He is a master, said by some to be a great master, in *karate** which is one of the Oriental bare-hand fighting systems— *aikido, judo, kempo*—which require half a lifetime to learn. Of all, the deadliest is *karate,* originated, legend says, by a Zen Buddhist priest called Daruma, around the year A.D. 500. The terrible power, the frightening quickness, of a master *karate*-player, are not quite credible until seen. Without at least photographic evidence, few may believe that a man can drive three fingers through a door as an arrow is driven through a straw target-matt, or cut a brick with his hand as a mason does with a hammer. In the ring with a heavy-weight champion of the world, Oyama would kill the man as soon as he was close enough to reach him. The boxer would have a rather better chance of survival if attacked by a gunman, because he might be able to take the gun away from his assailant. There is nothing to take away from Oyama, who knows that he can walk into a field and kill a bull with two blows, having done it. But no one could persuade Oyama to fight in earnest for money or show. It is the hope of *karate* masters that they will go through their entire lives without fighting in earnest. It is a matter of regret to Oyama that he was, some years ago, in Tokyo, twice assaulted, so suddenly and with such violence, once by one man with a bottle, once by four men with knives, that he reacted automatically and seriously injured them.

Listen to him speak: "Karate is not a game. It is not a sport, it is not even a system of self-defence. It is a way

*Pronounced ca-RAH-tay (Japanese 唐手 'Chinese art' or 'bare hands').

of learning to die. That is to say, it is a means of achieving serenity, tranquillity. Karate is half a physical exercise, and half a spiritual one. The karateist who has given the necessary years to exercise and meditation is a tranquil person. He has learned that every minute of life is a step towards death, and he is serene. In my life, I want to teach, and have people come with me in this useful art."

Watching Masutatsu Oyama execute one of the head-high leaps that are fundamental to *karate,* is one less moved than in watching Nureyev do the same? If so, the difference is in the context. Let Nureyev leap in the harsh cold morning light of the practice room in the *dojo*; let Oyama leap to music under the gauzed lights of Covent Garden. Is there in Oyama's leap less of artistry because it is harder to do than Nureyev's, require's greater strength and co-ordination, and is formed and justified by conviction learned in months of living alone in the mountains, standing by the hour under ice-cold waterfalls in meditation? Is one man less an artist than another because the mere overt purpose of his art is to kill or to run a motor-car thirteen times over the same forty-four miles of mountain roadway? And if, in pursuit of whatever inner vision drives one, one throws one's life into the hazard, does this make it a greater or a lesser thing? If a painter knew that he might be killed if his concentration flagged, and a brush rolled unheeded off his tabouret to the floor, would he be less an artist, or more? More, certainly, if he would go on, because a painter who can bring himself to do something else with his life than spend it painting is no real painter, using the word 'real' as Moss uses it in qualifying a 'real' driver or a 'real' professional. A 'real' artist, like a 'real' anything else, is driven, obsessed, dedicated, and he doesn't give a damn who or what is in his way.

And: no man ever lived, truly an artist, who was psychologically 'normal' or whose motivation could easily be understood by those around him. The ordinary housepainter finishes his work, has his pint and goes home to his wife. Vincent Van Gogh cut off his ear and gave it to a whore as a present. Ernest Hemingway put a goose-load into a shotgun, stuck the end of it into his mouth and plastered the top of his head against the ceiling for his wife to find. Achille Varzi, Nuvolari's rival and friend, a *grand prix* driver of the first rank, became so addicted to morphine in the middle 1930's that the German Auto-Union team had to terminate his contract.

Greatness does not come cheap. If it did, everyone would have some. The price is high, sometimes it is very high.

As Enzo Ferrari watched Nuvolari, fifty-seven years old and deathly sick, come through Modena in the *Mille Miglia* of 1948, he turned aside and wept. The bonnet had blown off Nuvolari's car, it was down on one side, a spring broken; Nuvolari was low in the chassis; he had thrown his broken seat overboard and was sliding around on a bag of oranges. He was leading the race in this wreck! He was running away from the likes of Ascari, Biondetti, Cortese; he was first by thirty-five minutes, with most of the race behind him, when the brakes went, a few miles past Modena, and he had nothing left to drive. Hollow-cheeked, trembling with fatigue, he let a priest lead him away to rest.

That year, and the year before it, there had been talk that some owners, some factories, did not care to have Nuvolari drive their cars. The man was too close to despair, they said, both of his sons, bright and handsome boys, dead in their teens, his own body a ruin. He was too old to drive, they said, and too much in agony to bear the solitude of retirement. 'He'll see a stone wall at the end of a long straight some day,' they said, 'he'll stand on the gas, and that will be that . . . but not, please God, in a car of mine.'

They were right in thinking that Nuvolari wanted to die. In the last years of his life, he often said so. But he was a devout Roman Catholic, and an Italian. He would not take his life, although he would insist upon his right to risk it, and risk it he did. Indeed, the mere effort of driving seemed to bring him close to collapse. His last *Mille Miglia,* and the one before, 1947, were thousand-mile-long defiances by a man who knew he had to finish the race to win, and therefore wanted to finish, but who obviously had left personal risk out of the equation. In 1947, driving a small and under-powered open Cisitalia roadster in a teeming rainstorm, he was nine minutes ahead of the veteran Clemente Biondetti, snug in a big closed Alfa-Romeo, at Bologna, on the home leg, when his roller-skate of a car ran through a puddle and drowned the ignition. In spite of a faulty diagnosis of the trouble by his mechanic, he was under way again in twenty minutes, and he finished second.

Nuvolari died in bed, on the 11th of August 1953, an irony if ever there was one. It is such rolls of life's apparently loaded dice that foster belief in fatalism. Determined to live up to his father's reputation for bravery, a legend in the United States Army, a man I know went from the Normandy beaches to Berlin, taking every mad chance that offered itself. By Berlin, there wasn't in his outfit one man whom he had known well the day he hit the beach—but he hadn't had so much as a skinned knuckle!

In warfare, very well, society is delighted to have you risk your life as much as you please, but in peacetime you must guard the right, and sometimes even fight for it. A strange thing. Life, liberty and the pursuit of happiness are the basic rights of man, and certainly inherent in the right to life is the right to give it up, either deliberately, in suicide, or by chance, in the risking of it. A United States senator, Richard Neuberger, a good man, one of the best, dead now, and his passing a loss, tried to outlaw automobile racing. He was an intelligent man, but still he believed that some men had the right, and ought to have the authority, to forbid other men to risk their lives. Stirling Moss's father, who had the authority and the right, was wise enough not to use it. He said, after the accident at Spa: "You can't ask a man to give up everything that makes his life worthwhile to him."

I hope not to hear again that someone intends to abolish motor-racing. On the other hand, I am opposed to the pretence that accidents never happen, and that whilst drivers may rarely die (their passing noted in the enthusiast journals —"Fatal accident mars race") they never do anything so vulgar as bleed. The purpose of this gambit, like the soothing lies that ring out over the public-address system after every accident, is apparently to prevent the authorities noticing that the sport is dangerous, lest they rouse themselves to legislate against it.

It is far better to fight on the line of the truth. "Grand Prix racing," Robert Daley has written, "is a deadly game. It always was and it always will be." That is a true statement. Racing should be defended, if it has to be defended, on that ground. It should be defended as what it is, a deadly game. Harmlessness is no protection against legislators running amok. In one place or another in the world it is illegal for a man to kiss his wife in public, to make love to her on Sunday, to drink beer, to plant a lawn, to ride a unicycle, all endeavours and pastimes one would think harmless to the community at large.

Surely we must govern our lives, we must govern our relations with each other, but I think the ideal rule a simple one: a man may risk his life in any way he pleases, so long as he does not cause other people *involuntarily* to risk theirs.

If a racing-car driver wants to do 130 miles an hour on a closed two-lane mountain circuit, that is his affair. If a man wants to stand beside the road in a bend, the better to see the car, that is his affair. If the driver loses the car, picks up the man and wraps the whole package around a tree, and ambulance people have to come and take them away to hospital or morgue, as the case may be, that is what they have been engaged for, and that is their affair. It is nobody's else.

CHAPTER XII

"It is good to begin well, but it is better to end well."

John Ray

CHAPTER XII

WHEN he knew how badly he had been hurt, how severely his brain had been damaged, when he found that he couldn't even open a door without giving himself step-by-step instructions—"I shall take the knob in my right hand, now I shall turn it sharply to the right, now I'll pull it"—Stirling Moss knew that he could not simply wait until the broken bones had mended and then go back to racing, as he had after the Spa accident in 1960. He knew that if his reaction-time and his vision did not return at least to normal, he could not drive a racing-car again. Further, he knew that if the doctors were correct in saying that whilst his reaction-time might improve rapidly, his vision would probably not be normal for two years or more, then there would be no point in it. He would be terribly out of practice and he would come wholly unprepared to the 1965 cars, having missed the 1962, '63, and '64 models. He decided that he must give himself a practical test, that as soon as he felt reasonably well, reasonably strong, he would take a racing-car to an isolated, completely closed circuit, and there, in privacy, try himself, and, on the basis of what he observed, make the decision, to go on or not, yes or no, then and there. As soon as he had settled on this plan, he announced it. He could set no date.

When he went to Nassau, immediately after being discharged from the Atkinson Morley Hospital, he drove a Mini-Minor, and he found that the island speed limit of thirty miles an hour suited him very well. When he returned to England he drove other cars, more quickly, but his re-training programme was interrupted by the two long stays in St. Thomas's for surgery. By January, 1963, his left eye now offering him correct focus as long as he looked straight ahead, he felt secure at 90–100 miles an hour on the road in his Lotus *Elite,* and it was impossible, riding with him, to detect slowness or lack of acuity. Everything seemed to be as before. He had the car completely in hand; he could drift it at will, he could do anything he pleased with it. But Moss allowed himself no enthusiasm, repeating what he had often said, that 100 on the road in a Lotus *Elite* has nothing whatever to do with 160 on a *grand prix* circuit in a Lotus 25.

He flew around the world. He had business commitments in South Africa, New Zealand and Australia and Hong Kong; he wanted to visit Tokyo; he had obligations in Day-tona and Nassau. Whilst he was away, he had asked Valerie Pirie to see to renewing his competition licence. He was back in England on February 26th, for ten days before going to the United States to fulfil a contract at Sebring. There was not enough time to engage a circuit and set up a car.

At noon on the 1st of May, Moss left London for Good-wood, where Ken Gregory and Tony Robinson were waiting for him with a Lotus. It had rained all morning, but the circuit was drying when Moss came to it, drying in places, deeply puddled in others. The loudspeakers were silent, but there must have been armies there for him, the mild May air must have rung with their shouts and with the howl of engines ripping across the flat land under the pale lemoned-coloured sun. The first significant British race-meeting after the war had been at Goodwood, in 1948, and Moss had won the 500 c.c. event, in his first Cooper. He was nineteen then. How many times he'd run at Goodwood

since, how many nights at the Fleece Inn, he couldn't begin
to remember.

He dropped himself into the car. It had occurred to him
that, coming out of Fordwater into St. Mary's for the first
time, running fast, some vagrant memory, the thin wedge
of a clue might come to him, something that would explain
the accident. No. It was just a bit of wet road. He felt
nothing.

He lapped the circuit for half an hour and more, running
fast but at his own rating at only around eight-tenths. At
the quickest, he said afterwards, he was three seconds over
what he would consider competitive time.

He had suspected what he would find, and he found it:
"I had to think," he said. "I had to give orders to myself:
here I'll brake, here I must change down, and so on . . .
and the other thing, I used to look at the rev-counter without
taking my eyes off the road, not only that, I could see the
rev-counter *and* the road *and* a friend waving to me, all
at the same time . . . I've lost that, that's gone."

He drove back to London. Ken Gregory called the press,
the bulletin went on the wires: "I've decided to retire. I
will not drive again." It was fifteen years, almost to the
day, from the date on which Stirling Moss had run his
Cooper up Prescott, in the Bugatti Owners Club event
which had been his first official competition.

1948

Date	Club	Event	Car (Type and Capaci
May 9	Bugatti Owners	Prescott Open Hill Climb	Cooper 497 c.c.
June 5	Brighton & Hove Motor Club	Stanmer Park Hill Climb	Cooper 497 c.c.
July 4	Blackburn Aircraft Motor Club	Brough	Cooper 497 c.c.
July 15	Jersey M.C. & L.C. Club	Bouley Bay International Hill Climb	Cooper 497 c.c.
			Cooper 497 c.c.
July 18	Bugatti Owners	Prescott Open Hill Climb	Cooper 497 c.c.
July 25	Hants & Berks	Great Aucklam Speed Trial	Cooper 497 c.c.
Aug. 7	West Hants & Dorset	Boscombe Speed Trials	Cooper 497 c.c.
Sept. 5	Brighton & Hove Motor Club	Brighton Speed Trials	Cooper 497 c.c.
Sept.12	Bugatti Owners	Prescott Hill Climb	Cooper 497 c.c.
Sept.18	B.A.R.C.	Goodwood	Cooper 497 c.c.
Sept.25	M.A.C.	Shelsley Walsh Hill Climb	Cooper 497 c.c.
Oct. 2	R.A.C.	Silverstone International Grand Prix 500 c.c.	Cooper 497 c.c.
Oct. 9	B.M.C.R.C.	Dunholme Lodge	Cooper 497 c.c.

1949

Date	Club	Event	Car (Type and Capaci
April 19	B.A.R.C.	Goodwood 2nd Easter Handicap	Cooper U/S 996
May 14	R.A.C.	British Grand Prix 500 c.c. National Race	Cooper 497 c.c.
May 26	B.R.D.C.	Isle of Man Manx Cup	Cooper U/S 996
May 28	West Hants & Dorset	Blandford Hill Climb	Cooper 497 c.c.
June 11	M.A.C.	Shelsley Walsh Hill Climb	Cooper U/S 996
June 25	Scottish Sporting Car Club Ltd.	Bo'ness Hill Climb	Cooper U/S 996
July 10	A.C. Brescia	IX circuito del Garda—Heat 1	Cooper U/S 996
		Final classification	
July 17	A.C. Rheims	French Grand Prix Formula B	Cooper U/S 996
July 21	Jersey M.C. & L.C. Club	Bouley Bay International Hill Climb	Cooper U/S 996
July 31	K.N.A.C. Zandvoort	Zandvoort 500 c.c. Race	Cooper 497 c.c.
Aug. 20	B.R.D.C.	Silverstone Daily Express International Meeting	Cooper 497 c.c.
Aug. 27	Lausanne A.C.	Prix du Léman Formula B	Cooper U/S 996
Sept. 11	Bugatti Owners	Prescott Hill Climb	Cooper U/S 996
Sept. 17	B.A.R.C.	Goodwood Madgwick Cup	Cooper U/S 996
Sept. 24	M.A.C.	Shelsley Walsh Hill Climb	Cooper U/S 996

1950

Date	Club	Event	Distance (miles)	Circuit	Formula	Car	Typ
April 10	B.A.R.C.	Easter Meeting (1st Event)	15	Goodwood	—	Cooper	110
		Third Easter Handicap	15	,,	—	H.W.M.	196
April 16	B.R. & S.C.C.	500 c.c. Races	20	Brands Hatch	III	Cooper	49
April 30	—	500 c.c. Paris G.P.	103	Montlhéry	III	Cooper	49

1948

Date	Result					Others	Time/Speed	Comments
	1st	2nd	3rd	4th	5th			
y 9	—	—	—	4th	—	—	51·01″	500 c.c. class racing cars F.T.D.
e 5	1st	—	—	—	—	—	58·78″	500 c.c. class racing cars.
y 4	1st	—	—	—	—	—	48·90 m.p.h.	Heat 3.
y 15	1st	—	—	—	—	—	58·00 m.p.h.	Handicap race.
,,	1st	—	—	—	—	—	63·80″	500 c.c. racing cars N.C.R. (new class record).
y 18	1st	—	—	—	—	—	49·51″	500 c.c. 16th. F.T.D.
y 25	1st	—	—	—	—	—	23·46″	500 c.c. class racing cars.
g. 7	1st	—	—	—	—	—	31·40″	500 c.c. class racing cars 2nd F.T.D.
t. 5	—	—	—	—	—	Sick motor	34·14″	500 c.c. class racing cars.
t. 12	—	—	3rd	—	—	—	53·67″	500 c.c. class racing cars. Fastest in Class.
t. 18	1st	—	—	—	—	—	71·92 m.p.h. 6′ ·04″	500 c.c. class racing cars, 3 laps 7·2 miles
t. 25	1st	—	—	—	—	—	43·84″	750 c.c. class racing cars
t. 2	—	—	—	—	—	Retired	—	Fastest practice lap 3′ 17·4″, 66·98 m.p.h. Blew up. Engine sprocket worked loose.
t. 9	1st	—	—	—	—	—	78·56 m.p.h. 22′ 36·4″	500 c.c. class racing cars, 8 laps 3·7 miles per lap.

1949

Date	Result					Others	Time/Speed	Comments
	1st	2nd	3rd	4th	5th			
il 19	1st	—	—	—	—	—	79·76 m.p.h. 9′ 41·6″	25″ start. Fastest lap 82·44 m.p.h.
y 14	1st	—	—	—	—	—	68·81 m.p.h. 44′ 26·2″	Fastest lap 70·95 m.p.h.
y 26	—	—	—	—	—	Retired	—	Engine failure—magneto.
y 28	1st	—	—	—	—	—	36·62″	500 c.c. class racing cars.
e 11	—	2nd	—	—	—	—	38·57″	1100 c.c. class racing cars.
e 25	—	2nd	—	—	—	—	36·1″	1100 c.c. class racing cars, 4th F.T.D.
y 10	—	—	3rd	—	—	—	1: 12′ 15·4″	1st of the 1100 c.c. class at 109·322 km.
,,	—	—	3rd	—	—	—	1: 30′	Broken chain.
y 17	—	—	—	—	—	Retired	—	
y 21	—	2nd	—	—	—	—	56·2″	1100 c.c. class racing cars, equal 3rd. F.T.D.
y 31	1st	—	—	—	—	—	66·92 m.p.h. 23′ 21·2″	Ten laps 41·93 km. Fastest practice lap.
g. 20	—	2nd	—	—	—	—	79·59 m.p.h. 22′ 22·6″	
g. 27	—	—	—	—	—	Retired	—	Engine trouble. Awarded Gold Cup for most meritorious performance.
t. 11	1st	—	—	—	—	—	44·77″	N.C.R.
t. 17	1st	—	—	—	—	—	8′ 46·2″ 82·10 m.p.h.	Fastest lap 84·7 m.p.h.
t. 24	1st	—	—	—	—	—	38·19″	

1950

Date	Result					Other Places	Time	Speed (m.p.h.)	Comments
	1st	2nd	3rd	4th	5th				
il 10	Hamilton	Moss	Bira	—	—	—	—	—	
,,	—	—	—	—	—	6th	—	—	
il 16	—	—	—	—	—	—	—	—	E/F. (seized piston).
il 30	—	—	—	—	—	—	—	—	E/F. (broken con rod).

1950—continued

Date	Club	Event	Distance (miles)	Circuit	Formula	Car	Type
May 13	B.R.D.C.	International 500 Race (Royal Silverstone)—Heat 1 Final	30	Silverstone	III	Cooper	497
May 14	A.C. de Mons	Belgian 'Prix de 500' Races	37	Mons (Coteaux Circuit)	II	H.W.M.	1960
May 20	A.C. de Monaco	Prix de Monte Carlo '500' Heat 1 Final	30	Monaco	III	Cooper	497
May 28	—	Aix les Bains 500 Race	—	Du Lac	III	Cooper	497
"	—	Aix les Bains Circuit	—	"	II	H.W.M.	1960
June 4	A.C. de Suisse	Swiss G.P.	—	Bremgarten	II	H.W.M.	1960
June 11	A.C. de Roma	Rome G.P.	—	Caracalla	II	H.W.M.	1960
June 25	B.R. & S.C.C.	500 c.c. Races (Open Challenge) Heat 1 Final	—	Brands Hatch	III	Cooper	497
"	"	500 c.c. Production Cars Heat 1 Final	—	"	"	"	"
July 2	—	'Coupe des Races 500'	63	Rheims	III	Cooper	497
"	—	'Coupe de Petites Cylindres'	126	"	II	H.W.M.	1960
July 9	—	Bari G.P.	200	Bari	I	H.W.M.	1960
July 22	—	Circuit of Posillipo—Heat 1	127	Naples	II	H.W.M.	1960
July 30	—	Geneva G.P.	112	Geneva	II	H.W.M.	1960
Aug. 7	Half Litre Club	'500' Trophy Races—Heat 2	35	Brands Hatch	III	Cooper	497
Aug. 12	Berne A.C.	Prix de Berne—Final	95	Bremgarten	II	H.W.M.	1960
Aug. 26	B.R.D.C.	International Trophy	101	Silverstone	I	H.W.M.	1960
"	"	500 c.c. Race	29	"	III	Cooper	497
Sept. 10	—	Circuit Mettet	98	Mettet	II	H.W.M.	1960
Sept. 16	R.A.C./U.A.C.	Tourist Trophy	—	Dundrod	Sports	Jaguar	3500
Sept. 17	Half Litre Club	500 c.c. Race—Heat	—	Brands Hatch	III	Cooper	497
Sept. 24	—	Circuit Perigeaux	85	Perigeaux	II	H.W.M.	1960
Sept. 30	B.A.R.C.	Race Meeting	—	Goodwood	II	H.W.M.	1960
"	"	"	—	"	III	Cooper	497
Oct. 7	Bristol C.C.	Castle Combe Races	—	Castle Combe	II	H.W.M.	1960
"	"	" —Heat	—	"	III	Cooper	497
"	"	"	—	"	Sports	Frazer Nash	2 lit
Oct. 15	—	Circuit of Garda	—	Lake Garda (Italy)	II	H.W.M.	1960
Oct. 24	Record Attempt	France	—	Montlhéry	Sports	Jaguar	3500
Nov. 17	M.C.C.	Daily Express Rally	—	G.B.	Sports	Aston-Martin DB2	

1951

Date	Club	Event	Circuit	Formula	Car	H.P.
Feb. 10	—	Chiltern Night Trial	—	Reliability Trials	Morris Minor	947 c
Mar. 26	B.A.R.C.	Lavant Cup	Goodwood	II	H.W.M.	1960 c
April 9	A.C. Marseille & Provence	Marseilles G.P.	Marseilles (240 km.)	—	H.W.M.	1960 c
April 22	—	G.P. San Remo	Aspedalette (189 km.)	—	H.W.M.	1960 c
April 28	—	Mille Miglia	Italy (1,000 miles)	Sports	Jaguar	3500 c

1950

Date	1st	2nd	3rd	4th	5th	Other Places	Time	Speed m.p.h.	Comments
ay 13	Moss	—	—	—	—	—	—	77·40	
	—	Moss	Collins	—	—	—	21' 53·8"	—	
ay 14	—	—	—	—	—	7th in Final	—	—	
ay 20	Moss	—	—	—	—	—	—	—	
	Moss	Schell	Parker	—	—	—	—	55·68	Fastest lap 2' 5·8". 56·55 m.p.h.
ay 28	—	—	—	—	—	—	—	—	Car did not finish (E/F.).
,,	—	—	—	—	—	—	—	—	
ne 4	—	—	—	—	—	—	—	—	Did not start due to illness.
ne 11	—	—	—	—	—	—	—	—	Car did not finish—broken stub axle.
ne 25	Moss	—	—	—	—	—	—	—	
	Moss	—	—	—	—	—	—	63·98	Fastest lap 65·94 m.p.h.
,,	Moss	—	—	—	—	—	—	—	
	Moss	—	—	—	—	—	—	63·31	Meeting Championship at 64·00 m.p.h.
ly 2	—	—	—	—	—	6th	—	—	One lap behind.
,,	Ascari	Simon	Moss	—	—	—	1: 17' 8·3"	—	
ly 9	Farina	Fangio	Moss	—	—	—	2: 36' 12·4"	—	Two laps behind.
ly 22	Moss	—	—	—	—	—	—	—	(Final) Did not finish, tyre burst.
ly 30	—	—	—	—	—	—	—	—	Did not finish.
ag. 7	Moss	—	—	—	—	—	—	—	
ag. 12	—	—	—	—	—	—	—	—	(Final) Did not finish, gearbox trouble. Fastest lap 67·67 m.p.h. (new record).
ag. 26	—	—	—	—	—	6th	—	—	
,,	Moss	—	—	—	—	—	—	79·87	
pt.10	Mayon	Moss	Macklin	—	—	—	—	—	
pt.16	Moss	—	—	—	—	—	—	—	
pt.17	Moss	—	—	—	—	—	—	—	
pt.24	Mayon	Simon	Moss	—	—	—	1: 52' 13·5"	—	
pt.30	—	—	—	—	—	7th	—	—	
,,	Dryden	Moss	—	—	—	—	—	—	Fastest lap at 72·39 m.p.h.
ct. 7	Moss	—	—	—	—	—	—	—	Did not finish in Final (E/F.).
,,	Moss	—	—	—	—	—	—	—	
,,	Moss	—	—	—	—	—	—	—	
ct. 15	—	—	—	—	—	—	—	—	Did not finish, broken stub axle.
ct. 24	—	—	—	—	—	—	—	—	New 24-hour record at 107·46 m.p.h.
ov. 17	—	—	—	—	—	—	—	—	Finished without penalty, but failed tests.

1951

Date	1st	2nd	3rd	4th	5th	Other Places	Time/Speed	Comments
eb. 10	—	—	—	—	—	—	—	Made a mess of map-reading.
ar. 26	Moss	—	—	—	—	—	—	
pril 9	Villoresi	—	Moss	—	—	—	2: ·05' 39·8"	
pril 22	Ascari	Villoresi	—	—	Moss	—	—	
pril 28	—	—	—	—	—	—	—	Accident (Moss/Johnson).

1951—continued

Date	Club	Event	Circuit	Formula	Car	H.F
May 3	A.C. Luxembourg	Luxembourg 500 G.P.	Fundel	III	Kieft	498
May 5	B.R.D.C./Daily Express	International Meeting General class.	Silverstone	I	H.W.M.	1960
" May 12	" Daily Telegraph	Production Car Race International Trophy 500 Race	" Brands Hatch	Sports —	Jaguar —	3500 —
May 13	—	Monza G.P. Race 1 Race 2 Final result	Monza	II	H.W.M.	1960
May 14	B.A.R.C.	International Trophy '500'—Final	Goodwood	III	Kieft	498
May 20	—	Columbian Centenary G.P.	Genoa	II	H.W.M.	1960
May 28	—	Swiss G.P.	Berne Bremgarten	I	H.W.M.	1960
June 4	A.C. de Savoie	Circuit Aix les Bains Heat 2 Final	Du Lac Aix les Bains	II	H.W.M.	1960
June 10	—	—	Rome	II	H.W.M.	1960
June 14	B.R.D.C./Daily Express	Empire Trophy	Isle of Man	Sports	Frazer Nash	1971
June 24	A.C. de l'Ouest	Le Mans 24-hours	Sarthe	Sports	Jaguar	3500
July 1	—	—	Avus	II	H.W.M.	1960
July 8	A.C. Normand	G.P. de Rouen	Rouen (Les Essarts)	II	H.W.M.	1960
July 14	B.R.D.C./R.A.C.	R.A.C. G.P. Britain	Silverstone	I	—	—
"	"	500 c.c. Race	" (60 miles)	III	Kieft-Norton	498
July 15	—	International Grand Trophy (210 miles)	Mettet (Belgium)	II	H.W.M.	1960
July 22	K.N.A.C.	Dutch G.P. (235 miles)	Zandvoort	I	H.W.M.	1960
" July 29	" A.C.V.D.	Dutch 500 c.c. Race German G.P.	" (44 miles) Nurburg Ring	III I	Kieft —	498 —
"	"	German 500 Race	"	III	Kieft	498
Aug. 5	Freiburg	Freiburg Hill Climb	Black Forest	III	Kieft	498
"	"	"	"	II	H.W.M.	1960
Aug. 11	Essex C.C.	Daily Mail Trophy	Boreham	—	—	—
"	"	500 c.c. Race	"	—	—	—
Aug. 12	Swiss A.C.	—	Erlen	II	H.W.M.	1960
Sept. 2	—	—	Bari	II	Ferrari	2000
Sept. 8	Irish M.R.C.	Wakefield Trophy	Curragh (Dublin)	II	H.W.M.	1960
"	"	O'Boyle Trophy	"	II	H.W.M.	1960
Sept. 15	R.A.C./Ulster A.C.	Tourist Trophy (Handicap Race) General class. Class 'C'	Dundrod (Belfast)	Sports	Jaguar	3500
Sept. 29	B.A.R.C.	Madgwick Cup	Goodwood	II	H.W.M.	1960
"	"	1st Sports Car Race	"	Sports	Jaguar	3500
"	"	2nd September Handicap	"	Sports	"	3500
"	"	3rd September Handicap	"	II	H.W.M.	1960
Oct. 6	Bristol M.C. & L.C.C.	—	Castle Combe	—	—	—
Oct. 13	Winfield Joint Committee	Winfield Races (Formula II)	Winfield (25 laps)	II	H.W.M.	1960
"	"	500 c.c. (Formula III)	"	III	—	—
Oct. 20	Half Litre Club	500 c.c. Races	Brands Hatch	III	Kieft	498
"	"	Open Challenge Race Heat 3 Final	"	"	"	"
"	"	Brands Hatch Championship Heat 2 Final	"	"	"	"

Date	Result					Other Places	Time/Speed	Comments
	1st	2nd	3rd	4th	5th			
ay 3	—	—	—	—	—	—	—	2 heats and final. Retired 5 laps.
ay 5	Moss	—	—	—	—	—	84·50 m.p.h.	1st over 2 litre Class.
"	—	—	—	—	—	6th Moss	—	
ay 12	—	—	—	—	—	—	—	Did not enter.
ay 13								
	—	—	—	Moss	—	—	—	
	—	—	Moss	—	—	—	1: 57′ 1·2″	
	—	—	Moss	—	—	—	—	Heat 1 retired E/F.
ay 14	Moss	—	—	—	—	—	—	
ay 20	—	—	—	—	—	—	—	Retired E/F.
ay 28	Fangio	—	—	—	—	8th Moss	2: 11′ 25″	
ne 4	Moss	—	—	—	—	—	1: 15′ 26·2″	Fastest lap (Heat 2) Moss, 101 k.p.h.
	Fischer	Moss	—	—	—	—	—	
ne 10	—	—	—	Moss	—	—	—	
ne 14	Moss	—	—	—	—	—	—	F.T.D.
ne 24	—	—	—	—	—	—	—	Lap record 167·662 k.p.h. 105·24 m.p.h. Retired 92 laps E/F.
ly 1	—	—	—	—	—	—	—	Retired E/F.
ly 8	—	—	—	—	—	—	—	Retired E/F.
ly 14	—	—	—	—	—	—	—	
	Moss	—	—	—	—	—	—	Fastest lap 2′ 2″: 85·23 m.p.h.
ly 15	Mayon	—	—	Moss	—	—	2: 19′: 90 m.p.h.	
ly 22	Rosier	Etancelin	Moss	—	—	—	—	
"	Moss	—	—	—	—	—	36′ 27·7″: 73 m.p.h.	(117·28 k.p.h.).
ly 29	—	—	—	—	—	—	—	
"	—	—	—	—	—	—	—	Fastest lap 72·7 m.p.h. Steering failure.
ag. 5	Moss	Wharton	—	—	—	—	—	
"	—	—	—	Moss	—	—	—	
ag. 11	—	—	—	—	—	—	—	
"	—	—	—	—	—	—	—	
ug. 12	—	—	—	—	—	—	—	Retired E/F. when in lead. (First drive in foreign car).
pt. 2	—	—	—	—	—	—	—	Retired—bad brakes.
pt. 8	Moss	Catherwood	Hamilton	—	—	—	1: 52′ 58·8″: 81·21 m.p.h.	Lap record 3′ 31·8″: 83·96 m.p.h.
"	Moss	—	—	—	—	—	—	
pt. 15	Moss	—	—	—	—	—	—	(S.M.M.T. Team Trophy Moss/Walker/Johnson)
	Moss	Walker	Gerrard	—	—	—	—	(& Greatest Distance 43 laps, 319 miles Moss)
pt. 29	Moss	Macklin	Abecassis	—	—	—	—	
"	Moss	—	—	—	—	—	—	
"	Moss	—	—	—	—	—	—	
"	Farina	Moss	—	—	—	—	—	
.t. 6	—	—	—	—	—	—	—	
ct. 13	Moss	Abecassis	Hamilton	—	—	—	37′ 1·7″: 81·1 m.p.h.	Fastest lap 82·1 m.p.h.
"	—	—	—	—	—	—	—	
t. 20								
"	Moss	—	—	—	—	—	65·86 m.p.h.	
	—	—	—	—	—	—	—	Did not start (cracked gear-box).
"	Moss	—	—	—	—	—	65·35 m.p.h.	
	Moss	—	—	—	—	—	66·91 m.p.h.	

1952

Date	Club	Circuit	Distance	Event	Formula	Car	H.P
Jan. 22	A.C. de Monaco	—	2,000 miles	Monte Carlo Rally	—	Sunbeam Talbot	2267
Feb. 17	Midland M.C.	—	—	Kitching Trophy	Speed Trial	Harford III	1172
Mar. 24	A.C. de Lyons	—	—	Lyons-Charbonnieres	—	XK120 Jaguar	—
April 12	Bristol M.C.	Castle Combe	10 laps	500 c.c. Race Heat 3 Final	III	Kieft	500
April 14	B.A.R.C.	Goodwood	6 laps	Earl of March Trophy	III	Kieft	500
„	„	„	6 laps	1st Easter Handicap	Sports	XK120C Jaguar	—
May 3	A.C. di Brescia	Road Race	1,000 miles	Mille Miglia	—	XK120C Jaguar	—
May 10	B.R.D.C.	Silverstone	15 laps	500 c.c. Race	III	Kieft	500
„	„	„	17 laps	Production Touring Cars	Saloon	Jaguar Mk. VII	3½ lit
„	„	„	17 laps	Production Sports Cars	Sports	Jaguar	—
„	„	„	5 laps	Race of Champions in XK120's	Sports	XK120 Jaguar	—
May 11	A.C. de Belgique	Bois de la Cambre	—	Brussels G.P.	III	Kieft	500
May 18	Berne A.C.	Berne	—	Swiss G.P.	II	H.W.M.	—
May 22	A.C. Luxembourg	—	58 miles	Luxembourg G.P.	III	Kieft	500
May 25	A.C.V.D.	Nurburg Ring	114 km.	Silver Jubilee Meeting	III	Kieft	500
„	„	„			II	H.W.M.	—
May 29	B.R.D.C.	Isle of Man	200 miles	Empire Trophy	Sports	Frazer-Nash	—
June 2	A.C. de Monaco	Monaco	—	Monaco G.P.	Sports	XK120C Jaguar	—
June 7	R.A.C./Ulster A.C.	Dundrod	34 laps	Ulster Trophy	Libre	B.R.M.	1½ lit super charg
June 14/15	A.C. de l'Ouest	Le Mans	—	24-hour Race	—	XK120C Jaguar	—
June 22	A.C. de Belgique	Francorchamps Spa	—	European G.P.	II	E.R.A.	2 lit
June 29	A.C. de Champagne	Rheims	—	—	Sports	XK120C Jaguar	—
„	„	„	—	French G.P.	II	H.W.M.	—
July 11	A.C. de Marseille	—	2,055 miles	Alpine Rally	—	Sunbeam Talbot 90	2 lit
July 19	B.R.D.C.	Silverstone	249 miles	British G.P.	II	E.R.A.	2 lit
„	„	„	45 miles	500 c.c. Race	III	Kieft	500
July 27	Welsh M.C.	Fairwood Airfield	—	500 c.c. Race	III	Kieft	500
Aug. 2	Essex C.C.	Boreham	67 laps	Daily Mail Trophy	II	E.R.A.	—
„	„	„	34 laps	Sports Car Race	Sports	XK120C Jaguar	3 lit
„	„	„	10 laps	500 c.c. Race	III	Cooper	500
Aug. 4	„	Brands Hatch	30 laps	Daily Telegraph International Trophy—Heat 3	III	Kieft	500
„	—	„	10 laps	August Sprint	III	Kieft	500
Aug. 5	—	Montlhéry	16,851·73 miles	Seven-Day Jaguar Records	—	XK120 Jaguar	3½ lit
Aug. 16	B.A.R.C.	Goodwood	283 laps	9-hour Sports Car Race	Sports	XK120C Jaguar	3 lit
Aug. 17	K.N.A.C.	Zandvoort	90 laps	Dutch G.P.	II	E.R.A.	—

1952

Date	1st	2nd	3rd	4th	Other Places	Speed	Time	Comments
Jan. 22	Allard	Moss	—	—	—	—	—	
Feb. 17	—	—	—	—	7th	—	—	
Mar. 24	—	Moss 2nd in Class	—	—	15th overall	—	—	
April 12								
	Moss	—	—	—	—	77·39 m.p.h.	—	Lap record 77·9 m.p.h.
	Moss	—	—	—	—	—	—	
April 14	Moss	—	—	—	—	78·07 m.p.h.	11' 4"	Fastest lap 79·56 m.p.h.
"	Holt	Swift	Duke	Moss	—	—	—	Fastest lap 82·60 m.p.h.
May 3	—	—	—	—	—	—	—	Retired.
May 10	Lewis-Evans	Brown	Moss	—	—	72·13 m.p.h.	36' 31"	Fastest lap 75·27 m.p.h.
"	Moss	—	—	—	—	75·22 m.p.h.	35' 32"	
"	Moss	—	—	—	—	84·02 m.p.h.	—	
"	Moss	—	—	—	—	—	—	
May 11	—	—	—	—	—	—	—	Retired—crash.
May 18	—	—	—	—	—	—	—	Retired.
May 22	—	—	—	—	6th	—	—	
May 25	—	—	—	—	—	—	—	Retired—crash.
"	Fischer	Moss	—	—	—	76 m.p.h.	—	
May 29	—	—	—	—	—	—	—	Retired—ignition.
June 2	—	—	—	—	—	—	—	Disqualified after pile-up.
June 7	—	—	—	—	—	—	—	Retired after 3 laps.
June 14/15	—	—	—	—	—	—	—	Retired—overheating.
June 22	—	—	—	—	—	—	—	Retired on 1st lap.
June 29	Moss	—	—	—	—	—	—	
"	—	—	—	—	10th	—	—	
July 11	Moss 1st in Class	—	—	—	—	—	—	
July 19	—	—	—	—	—	—	—	Retired—overheating.
"	—	—	—	—	—	82·50 m.p.h.	31' 46"	Fastest lap with Don Parker 84·98 m.p.h.
July 27	—	—	—	—	—	—	—	Retired—crash.
Aug. 2	Brown	Hawthorn	Moss	—	—	—	—	
"	Moss	—	—	—	—	88·09 m.p.h.	—	
" Aug. 4	Brown	Parker	Moss	—	—	—	—	
	Moss	—	—	—	—	67·90 m.p.h.	—	
"	—	Moss	—	—	—	—	—	Lap record 71·43 m.p.h.
Aug. 5	—	—	—	—	—	100·31 m.p.h. average	—	
Aug. 16	Moss 1st in Class	—	—	—	—	267 laps 71·09 m.p.h.	—	Rear axle.
Aug. 17	—	—	—	—	—	—	—	Retired on 74th lap when in 8th place.

1952—*continued*

Date	Club	Circuit	Distance	Event	Formula	Car	H.P.
Aug. 17	K.N.A.C.	Zandvoort	17 laps	500 c.c. Race	III	Cooper	500 c
Aug. 23	Scottish M.C.	Turnberry	—	Sports Car Race	Sports	XK120C	3 litr
				Heat 2		Jaguar	
				Final			
”	”	”	10 laps	500 c.c. Race	III	Cooper	500 c
Sept. 7	A.C. di Milano	Monza	—	Italian G.P.	II	Connaught	—
Sept. 27	B.A.R.C.	Goodwood	5 laps	500 c.c. Race	III	Cooper	500 c
”	”	”	5 laps	Sports Car Race	Sports	XK120C	—
						Jaguar	
”	”	”	—	Madgwick Cup	II	E.R.A.	—
Oct. 4	Bristol M.C.	Castle Combe		500 c.c. Race	III	Cooper	500 c
			7 laps	Heat 1			
			10 laps	Final			
”	”	”	20 laps	Racing Cars up to	II	E.R.A. G-type	—
				2000 c.c.			
Oct. 11	Winfield Joint Committee	Charterhall	20 laps	Sports Car Race	Sports	XK120C	—
						Jaguar	
”	”	”	25 laps	500 c.c. Race	III	Cooper/Norton	500 c
”	”	”	40 laps	Formula II Race	II	E.R.A.	—
Nov. 12	R.A.C./Daily Express	—	1,250 miles	Daily Express Rally	—	XK120 (closed)	3442 c
Dec. 2	—	—	3,352 miles	—	—	Humber Super Snipe	—

1953

Date	Club	Circuit	Distance	Event	Formula	Car	H.P.
Jan. 20	A.C. de Monaco	—	2,000 miles	Monte Carlo Rally	—	Sunbeam Talbot	—
Mar. 17	—	Jabbeke and Montlhéry	—	Sunbeam Alpine Records	—	Sunbeam Alpine	—
April 6	B.A.R.C.	Goodwood	7 laps	Lavant Cup	II	Cooper-Alta	—
”	”	”	—	Earl of March Trophy	III	Cooper	500 c
April 26	A.C. di Brescia	Road Race	1,000 miles	Mille Miglia	Sports	Jaguar	—
May 9	B.R.D.C./Daily Express	Silverstone		Trophy Race	II	Cooper-Alta	—
			15 laps	Heat 1			
			30 laps	Final			
”	”	”	17 laps	Production Touring Car Race	Saloon	Jaguar Mk. VII	—
”	”	”	17 laps	Production Sports Car Race	Sports	Jaguar	—
May 16	R.A.C./Ulster A.C.	Dundrod	10 laps	Ulster Trophy Heat 1	II	Connaught	—
May 25	Half-Litre Club	Crystal Palace	10 laps	500 c.c. Race	III	Cooper	500 c
”	”	”		Coronation Trophy	II	Cooper-Alta	—
			17 laps	Heat 1			
			10 laps	Final			
May 31	A.C.V.D.	Nurburg Ring	5 laps	German Motor Championship	III	Cooper-Norton	500 c
June 6	K.N.A.C.	Zandvoort	90 laps	Dutch G.P.	II	Connaught	—
June 13/14	A.C. de l'Ouest	Sarthe	—	Le Mans 24-hour Race	Sports	Jaguar	—

1952

Date	Result				Other Places	Speed	Time	Comments
	1st	2nd	3rd	4th				
ug. 17	Moss	—	—	—	—	75·15 m.p.h.	35' 21·5"	
ug. 23	Moss	—	—	—	—	—	—	
	Moss	—	—	—	—	—	—	
„	Moss	—	—	—	—	71·03 m.p.h.	14' 12"	
pt. 7	—	—	—	—	—	—	—	Retired on 46th lap when in 10th place.
pt. 27	Moss	—	—	—	—	79·24 m.p.h.	—	
„	Rolt	Moss	—	—	—	—	—	Fastest lap 85·37 m.p.h.
„	—	—	—	—	—	—	—	Retired.
ct. 4	Moss	—	—	—	—	—	—	
	Moss	—	—	—	—	—	—	Class record 80·58 m.p.h.
„	—	—	—	—	—	—	—	Retired—steering.
ct. 11	Stewart	Moss	—	—	—	76·09 m.p.h.	—	
„	Brandon	Moss	—	—	—	73·65 m.p.h.	—	
„	—	—	—	Moss	—	—	—	
ov. 12	—	—	—	—	13th overall	—	—	Class award.
ec. 2	—	—	—	—	—	—	—	15 countries in 3 days 18 hours.

1953

Date	Result				Other Places	Speed	Time	Comments
	1st	2nd	3rd	4th				
an. 20	—	—	—	—	6th	—	—	
ar. 17	—	—	—	—	—	120·459 m.p.h.	—	
pril 6	—	—	—	—	7th	—	—	
„	—	—	Moss	—	—	—	—	
pril 26	—	—	—	—	—	—	—	Retired.
ay 9	—	Moss	—	—	—	—	—	
	—	—	—	—	8th	—	—	
„	Moss	—	—	—	—	74·42 m.p.h.	—	Fastest lap 76·36 m.p.h. New lap record.
„	—	—	—	—	7th	85·67 m.p.h.	—	
ay 16	—	Moss	—	—	—	84·46 m.p.h.	—	N/S in final.
ay 25	Moss	—	—	—	—	68·26 m.p.h.	—	Fastest lap 70·68 m.p.h.
„	—	—	—	Moss	—	—	—	
	—	—	—	—	5th	—	—	
ay 31	Moss	—	—	—	—	66·55 m.p.h.	—	
une 6	—	—	—	—	9th	—	—	
une 13/14	Rolt Hamilton	Moss	—	—	—	—	—	

1953—continued

Date	Club	Circuit	Distance	Event	Formula	Car	H.P.
June 18	B.R.D.C.	Isle of Man	—	Empire Trophy Heat 3	Sports	XK120C Jaguar	—
			16 laps	Final			
June 28	A.C. Normand	Rouen	60 laps	Rouen G.P.	II	Cooper-Alta	—
July 5	A.C. de Champagne	Rheims	—	French G.P.	II	Cooper-Alta	—
„	„	„		12-hour Sports Car Race	Sports	XK120C Jaguar	—
July 10/16	A.C. de Marseille	—	1,947 miles	Alpine Rally	—	Sunbeam Alpine	—
July 18	B.R.D.C.	Silverstone	15 laps	500 c.c. Race	III	Cooper	500 c
July 26	A.C. of Portugal	Lisbon	—	Jubilee G.P.	Sports	Jaguar	—
Aug. 2	A.C.V.D.	Nurburg Ring	18 laps	German G.P.	II	Cooper-Jaguar	—
Aug. 9	—	Nantes	90 laps	G.P. des Sables d'Olonne	II	Cooper	—
Aug. 15	Winfield Joint Committee	Charterhall	20 laps	500 c.c. Race	III	Cooper	500 c
„	„	„	50 laps	Formula II Race	II	Cooper-Alta	—
„	„	„	50 laps	Formula Libre	II	Cooper-Alta	—
Aug. 22	B.A.R.C.	Goodwood	—	9-hour Race	Sports	Jaguar	—
Sept. 5	R.A.C.	Dundrod	823 miles	Tourist Trophy	Sports	Jaguar	—
Sept. 7	A.C. di Milano	Monza	—	Italian G.P.	II	Cooper-Alta	—
Sept. 19	Half-Litre Club	Crystal Palace	—	London Trophy Heat 1 Heat 2 Final	II	Cooper-Alta	—
„	„	„	—	Redex Challenge Trophy—Heat 1	III	Cooper	500 c
Sept. 20	Bugatti O.C.	Prescott	—	Hill Climb	II	Cooper-Alta	—
		„	—	„	Libre	Cooper	1100 c
Sept. 26	B.A.R.C.	Goodwood	7 laps	Madgwick Cup	II	Cooper-Alta	—
„	„	„	5 laps	Woodcote Cup	Libre II	Cooper-Alta	—
„	„	„	—	500 c.c. Race	III	Cooper	500 c
Oct. 3	Bristol M.C.	Castle Combe	—	Formula Libre	III	Cooper-J.A.P.	500 c

1954

Date	Club	Circuit	Distance	Event	Formula	Car	H.P.
Jan. 18	A.C. de Monaco	—	2,000 miles	Monte Carlo Rally	—	Sunbeam Talbot	—
Mar. 7	Sports Car Club of America	Sebring	170 laps	12-hour Sports Car Race	Sports	O.S.C.A.	1452 c
April 10	B.R.D.C./Cheshire Circuit Club	Oulton Park	20 laps	Empire Trophy Heat 1	Sports	Leonard-M.G.	—
May 9	—	Bordeaux	—	Bordeaux G.P.	I	Maserati 250F	—
May 15	B.R.D.C./Daily Express	Silverstone	15 laps	International Trophy—Heat 1	I	Maserati	—
„	„	„	—	Production Touring Car Race	Saloon	Jaguar Mk. VII	—
„	„	„	—	500 c.c. Race	III	Cooper	500 c
May 23	A.C.V.D.	Nurburg Ring	61 miles	International	III	Cooper-Norton	500 c

1953

Date	Result				Other Places	Speed	Time	Comments
	1st	2nd	3rd	4th				
ne 18	—	Moss	—	—	—	—	25' 33"	
	—	—	—	Moss	—	74·05 m.p.h.	54' 42"	
ne 28	—	—	—	—	10th	—	—	
ly 5	—	—	—	—	—	—	—	
„	Moss	—	—	—	—	104·69 m.p.h. average	—	
ly 10/16	—	—	—	—	—	—	—	Awarded the Coupe des Alpes.
ly 18	Moss	—	—	—	—	84·74 m.p.h.	—	Fastest lap 86·37 m.p.h. Did not start in G.P.
ly 26	—	Moss	—	—	—	—	—	
ıg. 2	Farina	Fangio	Hawthorn	Bonetto	6th	—	—	
ıg. 9	Rosier	Chiron	Moss	—	—	—	—	
ıg. 15	Moss	—	—	—	—	76·47 m.p.h.	—	
„	—	—	—	—	—	—	—	Retired.
„	—	—	—	—	—	—	—	Retired.
ug. 22	—	—	—	—	—	—	—	Retired.
pt. 5	—	—	Moss	—	—	81·71 m.p.h. average	9: 37' 12"	
ept. 7	—	—	—	—	13th	—	—	
ept. 19								
	Moss	—	—	—	—	70·68 m.p.h.	—	
	Moss	—	—	—	—	—	—	
	Moss	—	—	—	—	—	—	
„	Lewis-Evans	Moss	—	—	—	—	—	Retired in final.
ept. 20	Moss	—	—	—	—	46·48 m.p.h.	—	
„	—	Moss	—	—	—	46·35 m.p.h.	—	
ept. 26	Salvadori	Moss	—	—	—	—	—	
„	Hawthorn	Fangio	Wharton	Moss	—	—	—	
„	—	—	—	—	—	—	—	Retired.
ct. 3	—	—	—	—	—	—	—	Retired—crash.

1954

Date	Result				Other Places	Speed	Time	Comments
	1st	2nd	3rd	4th				
.n. 18	—	—	—	—	15th overall	—	—	Co-drivers Desmond Scannell and John Cooper.
ar. 7	Moss	—	—	—	—	73·6 m.p.h.	—	Co-driver Bill Lloyd.
³ril 10	—	—	Moss	—	—	—	40' 05"	Retired in final.
ay 9	—	—	—	Moss	—	—	—	
ay 15	—	—	Moss	—	—	—	32' 05"	Retired in final.
„	—	—	Moss	—	—	75·42 m.p.h.	39' 36"	Fastest lap 77·48 m.p.h. New record with Rolt and Appleyard.
„	Moss	—	—	—	—	84·21 m.p.h.	31' 5"	Fastest lap 86·37 m.p.h. with Leston.
ay 23	Moss	—	—	—	—	72·0 m.p.h. average	58' 49·8"	

1954—*continued*

Date	Club	Circuit	Distance	Event	Formula	Car	H.P.
May 29	B.A.R.C.	Aintree	17 laps	'200' Formula Libre Heat 1	I	Maserati	—
			34 laps	Final			
"	"	"	—	500 c.c. Race	III	Cooper	500 c
June 6	A.C. di Roma	Rome	60 laps	Rome G.P.	I	Maserati	—
June 12/13	A.C. de l'Ouest	Sarthe	—	Le Mans 24 hours	Sports	Jaguar	—
June 20	A.C. de Belgique	Francorchamps Spa	36 laps	Belgian G.P.	I	Maserati	—
July 4	A.C. de Champagne	Rheims	—	12-hour Sports Car Race	Sports	Jaguar	—
July 8	A.C. de Marseille	—	2,500 miles	Alpine Rally	—	Sunbeam Alpine	—
July 17	B.R.D.C./Daily Express	Silverstone	90 laps	British G.P.	I	Maserati	—
"		"	17 laps	500 c.c. Race	III	Cooper	500 c
July 25	A.C. de l'Ouest	Circuit de la Prairie	60 laps	Caen G.P.	I	Maserati	—
Aug. 1	A.C.V.D.	Nurburg Ring	22 laps	German G.P.	I	Maserati	—
Aug. 2	B.R.S.C.C./Daily Telegraph	Brands Hatch	10 laps	Daily Telegraph International Trophy—Heat 4	III	Cooper	500 c
			40 laps	Final			
Aug. 7	Cheshire C.C./Daily Dispatch	Oulton Park	36 laps	Gold Cup	I	Maserati	—
"		"	20 laps	Formula Libre	I	Maserati	—
"	"	"	27 laps	500 c.c. Race	III	Cooper	500 c
Aug. 15	A.C. di Pescara	Pescara	254 laps	Pescara G.P.	I	Maserati	—
Aug. 22	A.C. de Suisse	Bremgarten	66 laps	Swiss G.P.	I	Maserati	—
Sept. 5	A.C. di Milano	Monza	80 laps	Italian G.P.	I	Maserati	—
Sept. 11	R.A.C./Ulster A.C.	Dundrod	680 miles	Tourist Trophy	Sports	D-type Jaguar	2½ lit
Sept. 25	B.A.R.C.	Goodwood	21 laps	Goodwood Trophy	I	Maserati	—
"	"	"	5 laps	Sports Car Race	Sports	Lister-Bristol	1971 c
"	"	"	5 laps	500 c.c. Race	500 c.c.	Cooper	500 c
"	"	"	10 laps	Woodcote Cup—Formula Libre	I	Maserati	—
Oct. 2	B.A.R.C./Daily Telegraph	Aintree	17 laps	Daily Telegraph Trophy	I	Maserati	—
"	"	"	17 laps	Formula Libre Race	I	Maserati	—
"	"	"	17 laps	500 c.c. Race	III	Cooper-Norton	500 c
Oct. 10	—	Montlhéry	24 laps	Coupe du Salon 1½ litre Class	Sports	Connaught	1500 c
Oct. 24	—	Pedralbes Circuit	80 laps	Spanish G.P.	I	Maserati	—
Nov. 29	—	—	1,100 miles	American Mountain Rally	—	Sunbeam Alpine	—

Date	1st	2nd	3rd	4th	Other Places	Speed	Time	Comments
ay 29	—	—	Moss	—	—	—	40′ 12″	
„	Moss	—	—	—	—	77·70 m.p.h.	1: 18′ 48·4″	
„	Moss	—	—	—	—	70·92 m.p.h.	25′ 22·8″	
ne 6	—	—	—	—	6th	—	—	54 laps completed.
ne 12/13	—	—	—	—	—	—	—	Retired with brake trouble. Peter Walker co-driver.
ne 20	—	—	Moss	—	—	Average of 111·4 m.p.h.	2: 46′ 9″	35 laps completed.
ly 4	—	—	—	—	—	—	—	Retired—back axle.
ly 8	—	—	—	—	10th overall	—	—	Awarded Coupe des Alpes en Or. John Cuts as co-driver.
ly 17	—	—	—	—	—	—	—	Retired on lap 81 with broken drive shaft. Fastest lap 95·7 m.p.h. with Ascari–Fangio–Behra.
„	Moss	—	—	—	—	75·49 m.p.h.	—	
ly 25	Trintignant	Moss	—	—	—	—	—	Fastest lap 1′25·7″. Record.
ug. 1	—	—	—	—	—	—	—	Retired on 2nd lap—E/F.
ug. 2	—	—	—	—	—	—	—	
„	—	Moss	—	—	—	—	—	
ug. 7	—	Moss	—	—	—	—	42′ 19·4″	
„	Moss	—	—	—	—	83·48 m.p.h.	1: 11′ 27″	Fastest lap 85·11 m.p.h.
„	Moss	—	—	—	—	82·91 m.p.h.	39′ 58″	New record 85·40 m.p.h.
„	Moss	—	—	—	—	74·89 m.p.h.	59′ 43·8″	
ug. 15	—	—	—	—	—	—	—	Retired—oil pipe.
ug. 22	—	—	—	—	—	—	—	Retired on 21st lap—oil pipe drive.
pt. 5	Fangio	Hawthorn	Gonzales	—	10th	—	—	Retired on 71st lap when in lead. Split oil tank.
pt. 11	—	—	—	—	18th	—	—	Pushed over finish line. Oil pressure trouble. Co-driver Peter Walker.
pt. 25	Moss	—	—	—	—	91·49 m.p.h.	33′ 3·2″	Fastest lap 92·90 m.p.h.
„	—	Moss	—	—	—	—	8′ 46·6″	Fastest lap 83·72 m.p.h.
„	—	Moss	—	—	—	—	8′ 51·0″	Record lap 85·88 m.p.h.
„	—	—	Moss	—	—	—	15′ 48″	
ct. 2	Moss	—	—	—	—	85·43 m.p.h.	35′ 39″	Fastest lap with Hawthorn 86·54 m.p.h.
„	Moss	—	—	—	—	85·26 m.p.h.	35′ 53·4″	Record lap 89·55 m.p.h.
„	Moss	—	—	—	—	77·53 m.p.h.	39′ 28″	Fastest lap with Russell 78·72 m.p.h.
ct. 10	Moss	—	—	—	—	—	—	
ct. 24	—	—	—	—	—	—	—	Retired on lap 21. Scavenge pump failure.
ov. 29	Team Award	—	—	—	—	—	—	Co-driver Ron Kessel.

223

1955

Date	Club	Circuit	Distance	Event	Formula	Car	H.P.
Jan. 16	A.C. di Buenos Aires	Ottubre 17 Buenos Aires	96 laps	Argentine G.P.	I	Mercedes	—
Jan. 30	„	4·7 Lap Course of Autodrome	30 laps „	Buenos Aires G.P. Heat 1 Heat 2 Result	I	Mercedes	—
Mar. 13	—	Sebring	—	12-hour Sports Race	Sports	Austin Healey S	2660 c.c
April 11	B.A.R.C.	Goodwood	5 laps	Sports Car Race	Sports	Beart-Climax	1500 c.c
„	„	„	7 laps	Chichester Cup (Formula Libre)	I	Maserati	—
„	„	„	21 laps	Glover Trophy	I	Maserati	
April 24	A.C. de Bordeaux	Bordeaux	123 laps	Bordeaux G.P.	I	Maserati	—
Apr. 30/ May 1	A.C. di Brescia	Road Race	1,000 miles	Mille Miglia	Sports	Mercedes 300SLR	—
May 7	B.R.D.C./Daily Express	Silverstone	60 laps	Daily Express Trophy Race	I	Maserati	2492 c.c
May 22	A.C. de Monaco	Monaco	100 laps	European G.P.	I	Mercedes W196	—
May 29	A.C.V.D.	Nurburg Ring	10 laps	Eifelrennen	Sports	Mercedes 300SLR	—
June 5	A.C. de Belgique	Francorchamps Spa	36 laps	Belgian G.P.	I	Mercedes	2496 c.c
June 11/12	A.C. de l'Ouest	Sarthe	—	Le Mans 24-hour Race	Sports	Mercedes 300SLR	—
June 19	K.N.A.C.	Zandvoort	100 laps	Dutch G.P.	I	Mercedes	—
July 16	B.A.R.C./Daily Telegraph	Aintree	90 laps	British G.P.	I	Mercedes	—
July 24	A.C. de Portugal	Monsanto Cir., Lisbon	25 laps	Civil Governor Cup	Sports	Porsche Spyder	1500 c.c
Aug. 7	K.U.K. of Sweden	Råbelöv Circuit	32 laps	Swedish Sports Car G.P.	Sports	Mercedes 300SLR	2974 c.c
Aug. 13	West Essex C.C.	Snetterton	25 laps	Redex Trophy Race	I	Maserati	—
Aug. 20	B.A.R.C.	Goodwood	309 laps	9-hour Race	Sports	Porsche Spyder	1500 c.c
Aug. 27	B.R.S.C.C./Daily Herald	Oulton Park	80 laps	Daily Herald International Trophy Race 1500 c.c. Class	Sports	Connaught	1498 c.c
„	„	„	15 laps	Sporting Life Trophy	Saloon	Standard 10	—
Sept. 3	B.A.R.C./Daily Telegraph	Aintree	17 laps	Daily Telegraph Trophy	I	Maserati	—
Sept. 11	A.C. di Milano	Monza	50 laps	Italian G.P.	I	Mercedes	
Sept. 17	R.A.C./Ulster A.C.	Dundrod	84 laps	Tourist Trophy	Sports	Mercedes 300SLR	
Sept. 24	Cheshire M.C./ Daily Dispatch	Oulton Park	54 laps	Gold Cup	I	Maserati	—
Oct. 16	A.C. di Palermo	Road Race	13 laps	Targa Florio	Sports	Mercedes 300SLR	2974 c.c
Dec. 9/11	Bahamas A.C.	Nassau	30 laps	Governor's Trophy	Sports	Austin-Healey	—
„	„	„	60 laps	Nassau Trophy	Sports	Austin-Healey	—

1955

Date	Result				Other Places	Speed	Time	Comments
	1st	2nd	3rd	4th				
Jan. 16	—	—	—	Moss	—	—	—	4th with Kling and Herrmann. 94 laps completed.
Jan. 30	Farina	Fangio	Moss	—	—	—	1: 12′ 1·2″	
,,	Moss	Fangio	—	—	—	73·59 m.p.h.	1: 11′ 29·6″	Fastest lap with Farina—75·48 m.p.h.
,,	Fangio	Moss	Gonzales	—	—	—	2: 23′ 30·8″	
Mar. 13	—	—	—	—	6th	—	—	Co-driver Lance Macklin.
April 11	—	—	—	—	—	—	—	Retired on 3rd lap.
,,	—	—	Moss	—	—	—	11′ 20″	
,,	—	—	—	—	—	—	—	Retired on 13th lap.
April 24	—	—	—	Moss	—	—	2: 54′ 36·9″	Fastest lap 67·67 m.p.h.
April 30/	Moss	—	—	—	—	97·80 m.p.h.	10: 7′ 46″	Record.
May 1								
May 7	—	—	—	—	—	—	—	Retired on lap 11—cylinder head trouble.
May 22	—	—	—	—	9th	—	—	81 laps completed—pushed car over finish line to qualify.
May 29	Fangio	Moss	—	—	—	—	1: 44′ 53″	
June 5	Fangio	Moss	—	—	—	—	2: 39′ 37·1″	
June 11/12	—	—	—	—	—	—	—	Mercedes team withdrawn at 1.45 a.m.
June 19	Fangio	Moss	—	—	—	—	2: 54′ 24·1″	
July 16	Moss	Fangio	—	—	—	86·47 m.p.h.	3: 7′ 21·2″	Lap record of 89·70 m.p.h.
July 24	Moss	—	—	—	—	80·99 m.p.h.	1: 2′ 36·53″	Fastest lap of 83·53 m.p.h.
Aug. 7	Fangio	Moss	—	—	—	—	1: 18′ 14″	Fastest lap with Fangio 2′ 24·5″.
Aug. 13	—	—	Moss	—	—	—	50′ 26″	Fastest lap 83·79 m.p.h.
Aug. 20	—	—	—	—	—	—	—	Retired on lap 237 after collision with Crook. Co-driver von Hanstein.
Aug. 27	—	—	—	—	7th overall	78·34 m.p.h.	2: 44′ 56·4″	Completed 78 laps.
	Moss	—	—	—	—	—	—	
,,	—	Moss	—	—	—	62·79 m.p.h.	36′56·2″	Completed 14 laps.
Sept. 3	—	—	—	—	—	—	—	Retired on 13th lap.
Sept. 11	—	—	—	—	—	—	—	Retired on 28th lap—transmission trouble. Fastest lap 134·04 m.p.h.
Sept. 17	Moss	—	—	—	—	88·32 m.p.h.	7: 3′ 11″	Co-driver John Fitch.
Sept. 24	Moss	—	—	—	—	85·94 m.p.h.	1: 44′ 5·4″	Record lap 87·81 m.p.h.
Oct. 16	Moss	—	—	—	—	59·80 m.p.h.	9: 43′ 14″	Co-driver Peter Collins. Fastest lap—Moss 43′ 7·4″, 62·2 m.p.h.
Dec. 9/11	—	—	—	—	6th	—	—	
,,	—	—	—	—	—	—	—	Retired.

1956

Date	Club	Circuit	Distance	Event	Formula	Car	H.P.
Jan. 7	N.Z.I.G.P.	Ardmore	210 miles 100 laps	New Zealand G.P.	I	Maserati 250F	—
"	"	"	31·5 miles 15 laps	Ardmore Handicap Race	Sports	Porsche Spyder	—
Jan. 22	Automovil Club Argentina	Buenos Aires	238·25 miles 98 laps	Argentine G.P.	I	Maserati	—
Jan. 29	"	"	625·4 miles 106 laps	Buenos Aires 1,000 km.	Sports	Maserati	3 litre
Feb. 5	"	Mendoza	60 laps	Buenos Aires G.P.	I	Maserati	—
Mar. 24	Sports Car Club of America	Sebring	194 laps	12-hour Sports Car Race	Sports	Aston-Martin DB3S	2922 c.c.
April 2	B.A.R.C.	Goodwood	32 laps	Glover Trophy	I	Maserati	2497 c.c.
"	"	"	15 laps	Sports Car Race	Sports	Aston-Martin DB3S	2922 c.c.
April 14	B.R.D.C.	Oulton Park	44·17 miles 16 laps	British Empire Trophy—Heat 1	Sports	Cooper-Climax	1460 c.c.
"	"	"	69 miles 25 laps	Final			
April 23	B.A.R.C.	Aintree	201 miles 67 laps	Aintree '200'	I	Maserati	2497 c.c.
"	"	"	30 miles 8 laps	Sports Car Race	Sports	Cooper-Climax	1460 c.c.
April 28/29	A.C. di Bologna	Road Race	1,000 miles	Mille Miglia	Sports	Maserati	3½ litre
May 5	B.R.D.C.	Silverstone	174 miles 60 laps	Daily Express Trophy	I	Vanwall	2490 c.c.
"	"	"	72·50 miles 25 laps	Sports Car Race	Sports	Aston-Martin DB3S	2922 c.c.
May 13	A.C. de Monaco	Monte Carlo	195·4 miles 100 laps	Monaco G.P.	I	Maserati	2497 c.c.
May 21	B.R.S.C.C.	Crystal Palace	10 laps	London Trophy Part 1 Part 2	Libre	Maserati	2497 c.c.
"	"	"	10 laps	Anerley Trophy	Sports	Cooper-Climax	1496 c.c.
"	"	"	10 laps	Norbury Trophy	Sports	Cooper-Climax	1496 c.c.
May 27	A.D.A.C.	Nurburg Ring	44 laps	Nurburg Ring 1,000 km.	Sports	Maserati	2988 c.c.
June 3	R.A.C. de Belgique	Francorchamps Spa	36 laps	Belgian G.P.	I	Maserati	2497 c.c.
June 24	A.C. de Milano	Monza	1,000 km. 100 laps	Lotteria di Monza	Sports	Maserati	2000 c.c.
July 1	A.C. de Champagne	Rheims	1,226·39 miles	12-hour Sports Car Race	Sports	Cooper-Climax	1460 c.c.
"	"	"	514·699 miles 61 laps	French G.P.	I	Maserati	2497 c.c.
July 8	A.C. de Normand	Rouen Les-Essarts	205 miles 50 laps	Rouen G.P.	Sports	Aston-Martin	—
July 14	B.R.D.C.	Silverstone	303 miles 101 laps	British G.P.	I	Maserati	2497 c.c.
"	"	"	25 laps	Sports Car Race	Sports	Maserati	3 litre
July 22	A.C. di Bari	Bari	124·29 miles 36 laps	Bari G.P.	Sports	Maserati	3 litre
July 28/29	A.C. de l'Ouest	Sarthe	299 laps	Le Mans 24-hour Race	Sports	Aston-Martin DB3S	2922 c.c.
Aug. 5	A.C.V.D.	Nurburg Ring	22 laps	German G.P.	I	Maserati	2497 c.c.
"	"	"	7 laps	1½-litre Sports Car Race	Sports	Maserati	—
Aug. 12	—	Råbelöv	153 laps	Swedish G.P.	Sports	Maserati	2988 c.c.

1956

Date	Result				Other Places	Speed	Time	Comments
	1st	2nd	3rd	4th				
Jan. 7	Moss	—	—	—	—	78·40 m.p.h.	2: 32' 43·1"	
„	Moss	—	—	—	—	71·20 m.p.h.	29' 59·8"	Handicap 4' 47".
Jan. 22	—	—	—	—	—	—	—	Retired on lap 82 when leading from 43rd lap. E/F.
Jan. 29	Moss	—	—	—	—	96·11 m.p.h.	6: 29' 37·9"	Co-driver Menditeguy.
Feb. 5	—	Moss	—	—	—	—	1: 53' 17"	
Mar. 24	—	—	—	—	—	—	—	Retired lap 51—transmission. Co-driver Collins.
April 2	Moss	—	—	—	—	94·35 m.p.h.	48' 50·4"	Fastest lap 1' 30·2", 95·79 m.p.h.
„	Moss	—	—	—	—	89·18 m.p.h.	24' 13·2"	Fastest lap 1' 35", 90·95 m.p.h.
April 14	—	—	—	Moss	—	—	32' 4"	Fastest lap 1' 58", 84·23 m.p.h.
„	Moss	—	—	—	—	83·72 m.p.h.	49' 28"	Fastest lap 1' 57", 84·95 m.p.h.
April 23	Moss	—	—	—	—	82·24 m.p.h.	2: 23' 6·4"	
„	—	—	—	—	5th	—	18' 6·2"	
April 28/29	—	—	—	—	—	—	—	Retired 5 minutes out of Pescara—front wheels locked—crashed.
May 5	Moss	—	—	—	—	100·47 m.p.h.	1: 44' 55"	Lap record 1'43", 102·30 m.p.h.—14 times.
„	—	Moss	—	—	—	84·79 m.p.h.	46' 19"	
May 13	Moss	—	—	—	—	64·95 m.p.h.	3: 0' 32·9"	
May 21								
	Moss	—	—	—	—	73·91 m.p.h.	11' 13·0"	Fastest lap 1' 5".
	Moss	—	—	—	—	74·31 m.p.h.	11' 13·4"	Fastest lap 1' 2·6", 79·94 m.p.h. (record).
„	—	Moss	—	—	—	—	11' 15"	
„	Moss	—	—	—	—	75·55 m.p.h.	11' 2·4"	Fastest lap 1' 4·8", 77·22 m.p.h. (record).
May 27	Moss	—	—	—	—	80·40 m.p.h.	7: 43' 54·5"	Drivers: Behra, Taruffi, Schell.
June 3	—	—	Moss	—	—	115·99 m.p.h.	2: 43' 16·9"	Nearside rear wheel and brake drum came off when 2nd. Took over Perdisa's car to finish 3rd. Lap record: 4' 14·7", 124·15 m.p.h.
June 24	—	Moss	—	—	—	—	5: 7' 40·7"	
July 1	—	—	—	—	—	—	—	Retired after 30 minutes. Fastest lap 2' 45·3", 112·16 m.p.h.
„	—	—	—	—	5th	—	2: 35' 1·5"	Retired lap 22—broken gear lever. Took over Perdisa's car. 59 laps completed.
July 8	—	Moss	—	—	—	—	2: 10' 35"	
July 14	—	—	—	—	—	—	—	Led from start to lap 68, thereafter 2nd until retirement lap 94—fuel tank leak. Fastest lap 1' 43·2", 102·104 m.p.h.
„	Moss	—	—	—	—	93·94 m.p.h.	46' 44"	Fastest lap 1' 49", 96·67 m.p.h.
July 22	Moss	—	—	—	—	81·92 m.p.h.	1: 50' 52·4"	Fastest lap 2' 28·9", 83·11 m.p.h.
July 28/29	—	Moss	—	—	—	104·04 m.p.h.	—	Co-driver Peter Collins. 298 laps completed.
Aug. 5	—	Moss	—	—	—	—	3: 39' 30·1"	
„	—	Moss	—	—	—	—	1: 13' 29·8"	Fastest lap 10' 13·3", 83·2 m.p.h.
Aug. 12	—	—	—	—	—	—	—	Car burnt out at pits. Co-driver Behra.

1956—*continued*

Date	Club	Circuit	Distance	Event	Formula	Car	H.P.
Aug. 18	B.R.S.C.C./Daily Herald	Oulton Park	40 laps	Daily Herald International Trophy	Sports	Aston-Martin DB3S	2922 c.c
,,	,,	,,	10 laps	Sporting Life Trophy	Sports	Cooper-Climax	1460 c.c.
Sept. 2	A.C. di Milano	Monza	50 laps	Italian G.P.	I	Maserati	2467 c.c
Sept. 17/23	F.F.S.A. and R.S.A.C. Nice	—	—	Tour de France	G.T.	Mercedes 300SL	—
Nov. 4	A.C. de Venezuela	Caracas	85 laps	Venezuela G.P.	Sports	Maserati	3 litre
Nov 25	Confederation of Australian Motor Sport	Albert Park	100·16 miles 32 laps	Australian Tourist Trophy	Sports	Maserati	2992 c.c.
Dec. 2	,,	,,	248 miles 80 laps	Australian G.P.	I	Maserati	2497 c.c.
Dec. 9	Bahamas A.C.	Nassau	210 miles 60 laps	Nassau Trophy	Sports	Maserati 300S	—

1957

Date	Club	Circuit	Distance	Event	Formula	Car	H.P.
Jan. 13	Automovil Club Argentina	Buenos Aires	100 laps	Argentine G.P.	I	Maserati 250	—
Jan. 20	,,	,,	98 laps	Buenos Aires 1,000 km.	Sports	Maserati	3 litre
Jan. 27	,,	Circuit No. 4 of Autodrome	30 laps	Buenos Aires G.P. Heat 1	—	—	—
,,				2nd and final Heat			
Feb. 25	Automovil y Aero Club de Cuba	Havana	90 laps	Cuban G.P.	Sports	Maserati	2 litre
Mar. 24	S.C.C.A.	Sebring	197 laps	Sebring 12-hours	Sports	Maserati	3 litre
April 7	A.C. di Siracusa	Syracuse	80 laps	Syracuse G.P.	I	Vanwall	—
April 22	B.A.R.C.	Goodwood	32 laps	Richmond Trophy	I	Vanwall	—
May 12	A.C. di Brescia	Road Race	1,000 miles	Mille Miglia	Sports	Maserati	4¼ litre
May 19	A.C. de Monaco	Monte Carlo	105 laps	Monaco G.P.	I	Vanwall	—
May 26	A.D.A.C.	Nurburg Ring	44 laps	Nurburg Ring 1,000 km.	Sports	Maserati	4¼ litre
June 22/23	A.C. de l'Ouest	Sarthe	24-hours	Le Mans	Sports	Maserati Coupe	4¼ litre
July 20	B.A.R.C.	Aintree	90 laps	British G.P. (European G.P.)	I	Vanwall	—
Aug. 4	A.C.V.D.	Nurburg Ring	22 laps	German G.P.	I	Vanwall	—
Aug. 11	—	Kristianstad	145 laps	Swedish G.P.	Sports	Maserati	4¼ litre
Aug. 18		Pescara	18 laps	Pescara G.P.	I	Vanwall	—
Aug. 23		Utah		Record Attempt	—	M.G.	—
Sept. 8	A.C. di Milano	Monza	87 laps	Italian G.P.	I	Vanwall	—
Sept. 15	—	—	3,400 miles	Tour de France	G.T.	Mercedes 300SL	—
Oct. 27	R.A.C. Marocain	Casablanca	—	Moroccan G.P.	I	Vanwall	—
Nov. 3	A.C. de Venezuela	Caracas	101 laps	Venezuela G.P.	Sports	Maserati	4¼ litre
Dec. 8	Bahamas A.C.	Nassau	—	Nassau Trophy	—	Ferrari	3½ litre
,,	,,	,,	—	Nassau Tourist Trophy	Sports	Aston-Martin	

1956

Date	Result				Other Places	Speed	Time	Comments
	1st	2nd	3rd	4th				
Aug. 18	Moss	—	—	—	—	76·99 m.p.h.	1: 26′ 3·8″	Fastest lap 2′ 6·8″, 78·39 m.p.h.
,,	Moss	—	—	—	—	75·69 m.p.h.	21′ 53·2″	Fastest lap 2′ 8·45″, 77·41 m.p.h.
Sept. 2	Moss	—	—	—	—	129·75 m.p.h.	2: 28′ 41·3″	Fastest lap 2′ 45·5″, 135·4 m.p.h.
Sept. 17/23	—	Moss	—	—	—	—	—	Co-driver Houel.
Nov. 4	Moss	—	—	—	—	84·33 m.p.h.	2: 31′ 49·8″	Fastest lap 1′ 39·7″, 85·53 m.p.h.
Nov. 25	Moss	—	—	—	—	94·65 m.p.h.	1: 3′ 24·2″	Lap record 1′ 55·8″.
Dec. 2	Moss	—	—	—	—	95·90 m.p.h.	2: 36′ 15·4″	Lap record 1′ 52·8″, 100·26 m.p.h.
Dec. 9	Moss	—	—	—	—	96·21 m.p.h.	2: 10′ 57″	Borrowed car from Bill Lloyd.

1957

Date	Result				Other Places	Speed	Time	Comment
	1st	2nd	3rd	4th				
Jan. 13	—	—	—	—	8th	—	—	Fastest lap 1′ 44·7″, 83·6 m.p.h. on lap 75.
Jan. 20	—	Moss	—	—	—	—	6: 11′ 53·4″	Fastest lap 3′ 36″, 105·95 m.p.h. Shared car with Behra and Menditeguy.
Jan. 27	—	—	—	—		—	—	Retired on lap 23, but classified as finisher.
	—	—	—	—	6th	—	2: 26′ 8″	Took over Menditeguy's car for final laps. 6th in classification.
Feb. 25	—	—	—	—	—	—	—	Retired after 22 laps—E/F.
Mar. 24	—	Moss	—	4th in Index	—	—	—	Co-driver Schell. 195 laps completed.
April 7	—	—	Moss	—	—	—	2: 40′ 48·1″	New lap record 1′ 54·3″, 107·39 m.p.h. 77 laps completed.
April 22	—	—	—	—	—	—	—	Retired lap 13—throttle linkage failure.
May 12	—	—	—	—	—	—	—	Retired 7½ miles from start—brake pedal broke.
May 19	—	—	—	—	—	—	—	Pile-up on lap 4—Hawthorn and Collins.
May 26	—	—	—	—	5th	—	—	Drivers—Godia, Gould and Fangio. Fastest lap 9′ 49·9″, 86·43 m.p.h. 43 laps completed.
June 22/23	—	—	—	—	—	—	—	Retired on lap 39—transmission.
July 20	Moss	—	—	—	—	86·80 m.p.h.	3: 6′ 37·8″	Changed cars with Brooks on lap 27. Lap record 1′ 59·2″, 90·60 m.p.h.
Aug. 4	—	—	—	—	5th	—	3: 35′ 15·8″	
Aug. 11	Moss	—	Moss	—	—	97·88 m.p.h.	—	Shared honours with Behra—handed over car to him when in lead. Took another to finish 3rd—3 litre.
Aug. 18	Moss	—	—	—	—	95·55 m.p.h.	2: 59′ 22·7″	Lap record 9′ 44·6″, 97·87 m.p.h.
Aug. 23	—	—	—	—	—	—	—	M.G. record attempt at Utah. Setting five new Class 'F' records.
Sept. 8	Moss	—	—	—	—	120·28 m.p.h.	2: 35′ 3·9″	
Sept. 15	—	—	—	—	5th	—	—	Co-driver Peter Garnier.
Oct. 27	—	—	—	—	—	—	—	Non-starter—'flu.
Nov. 3	—	—	—	—	—	—	—	Fastest lap 3′ 38″. Crash with Dressel when nearly 2′ in lead. Retired.
Dec. 8	Moss	—	—	—	—	101·603 m.p.h.	—	Borrowed car. Aston wrecked by Ruth Levy.
,,	—	—	—	—	24th	—	—	Lost 3rd place—fuel pump trouble.

1958

Date	Club	Circuit	Distance	Event	Formula	Car	H.P.
Jan. 19	Automovil Club Argentina	Buenos Aires	80 laps 194·4 miles	Argentine G.P.	I	Cooper	1960 c.c
Jan. 26	"	"	106 laps 1,000 km.	Buenos Aires 1,000 km.	Sports	Porsche	1581 c.c
Feb. 2	"	"	88·71 miles	Buenos Aires G.P.	I	Cooper	1960 c.c
Feb. 23	Automovil y Aero Club de Cuba	Havana	—	Cuban G.P.	Sports	Ferrari	4·1 litre
Mar. 22	Automobile Club of Florida	Sebring	200 laps	Sebring 12-hour	Sports	Aston-Martin DBR1	2922 c.c
April 7	B.A.R.C.	Goodwood	21 laps	Sussex Trophy	Sports	Aston-Martin DBR2	3910 c.c
"	"	"	42 laps	Glover Trophy	I	Cooper	1960 c.c
April 12	B.R.D.C.	Oulton Park	— 20 laps 25 laps	British Empire Trophy—Heat 3 Final	Sports	Aston-Martin DBR2	3910 c.c
April 19	B.A.R.C.	Aintree	67 laps 201 miles	Aintree '200'	I	Cooper	1960 c.c
May 3	B.R.D.C.	Silverstone	25 laps	Sports Car Race	Sports	Aston-Martin DBR3	2990 c.c
"	"	"	50 laps	Daily Express Trophy	I	Cooper	1960 c.c
May 11	S.I.A.T.S.	Sicily	—	Targa Florio	Sports	Aston-Martin DBR1	2922 c.c
May 18	A.C. de Monaco	Monte Carlo	100 laps 199 miles	Monaco G.P.	I	Vanwall	2496 c.c
May 26	K.N.A.C.	Zandvoort	75 laps 195 miles	Dutch G.P.	I	Vanwall	2496 c.c
June 1	A.D.A.C.	Nurburg Ring	44 laps	Nurburg Ring 1,000 km.	Sports	Aston-Martin DBR1	2922 c.c
June 15	R.A.C. de Belgique	Francorchamps Spa	24 laps	Belgian G.P.	I	Vanwall	2496 c.c
June 21	A.C. de l'Ouest	Sarthe	24-hours	Le Mans	Sports	Aston-Martin DBR1	2922 c.c
June 29	A.C. di Milano	Monza	62 laps 500 miles	Prix Esso—Heat 1	Libre	Maserati-Eldorado Special	4½ litre
"	"	"	62 laps	Prix Mobil—Heat 2	"	"	"
July 6	A.C. de Champagne	Rheims	30 laps	Coupe de Vitesse	II	Cooper	2014 c.c
"	"	"	50 laps	French G.P.	I	Vanwall	2496 c.c
July 13	A.C. di Portugal	Vila Real	35 laps	Vila Real	Sports	Maserati	2984 c.c
July 19	R.A.C./B.R.D.C.	Silverstone	75 laps 255 miles	British G.P.	I	Vanwall	2496 c.c
"	"	"	25 laps 75·25 miles	Sports Car Race	Sports	Lister-Jaguar	3781 c.c
July 20	A.C. de l'Ouest	Caen	86 laps 188·25 miles	Caen G.P.	I	Cooper	2014 c.c
Aug. 3	A.C.V.D.	Nurburg Ring	15 laps	German G.P.	I	Vanwall	2496 c.c
Aug. 10	Karlskoga M.C.	Karlskoga	50 laps	Karlskoga G.P.	Sports	Maserati	2984 c.c
Aug. 15	Automobil Sports Klubben	Roskilde Ring	16 laps	Copenhagen G.P.	Sports	Maserati	2984 c.c
Aug. 24	A.C. di Portugal	Oporto	50 laps 230 miles	Portuguese G.P.	I	Vanwall	2496 c.c
Aug. 30	B.R.S.C.C.	Brands Hatch	42 laps	Kentish '100' Heat 1 Heat 2	II	Cooper	1496 c.c
Sept. 7	A.C. di Italia	Monza	70 laps 249·2 miles	Italian G.P.	I	Vanwall	2496 c.c
Sept. 13	R.A.C./B.A.R.C.	Goodwood	148 laps 355·2 miles	Tourist Trophy	Sports	Aston-Martin DBR1	2992 c.c

Date	Result				Other Places	Speed	Time	Comments
	1st	2nd	3rd	4th				
Jan. 19	Moss	—	—	—	—	83·57 m.p.h.	2: 19' 37·7"	
Jan. 26	—	—	Moss	—	—	97·68 m.p.h.	6: 23' 17·8"	633·88 miles. 1st in class. 3rd overall.
Feb. 2	—	—	—	—	—	—	—	Retired.
Feb. 23	Moss	—	—	—	—	—	—	Fastest lap. Race called off after 5 laps —crash.
Mar. 22	—	—	—	—	—	—	—	Retired 90th lap—transmission failure. Co-driver Brooks. Record lap 3' 20·3", 93·6 m.p.h.
April 7	Moss	—	—	—	—	89·94 m.p.h.	—	Record lap 1' 33·4", 92·5 m.p.h.
„	—	—	—	—	—	—	—	Retired on lap 22. Record lap 1' 50·8", 89·7 m.p.h.
April 12	Moss	—	—	—	—	87·53 m.p.h.	—	
„	Moss	—	—	—	—	87·45 m.p.h.	—	Equalled lap record–1'50·8", 89·7 m.p.h.
April 19	Moss	—	—	—	—	85·66 m.p.h.	2: 20' 47"	
May 3	—	—	—	—	—	—	—	Retired 14th lap—E/F. Fastest lap during practice 1' 46". First 3-litre car to lap over 100 m.p.h.
„	—	—	—	—	—	—	—	Retired—gear box.
May 11	—	—	—	—	—	—	—	Retired on 5th lap—transmission failure. Co-driver Brooks. Record lap 42' 17·5", 63·33 m.p.h.
May 18	—	—	—	—	—	—	—	Retired lap 38—bent valve.
May 26	Moss	—	—	—	—	93·96 m.p.h.	2: 4' 49·2"	Fastest lap 1' 38·9", 94·84 m.p.h. on lap 32.
June 1	Moss	—	—	—	—	84·26 m.p.h.	7: 23' 33"	Co-driver Brabham. Record lap 9' 43", 87·5 m.p.h.
June 15	—	—	—	—	—	—	—	Retired 1st lap—over-revved engine.
June 21	—	—	—	—	—	—	—	Retired lap 30—E/F. Co-driver Brabham.
June 29	—	—	—	Moss	—	—	—	Retired after crash in final 3rd heat.
„	—	—	—	—	5th	—	1: 0' 35·1"	7th in general classification.
July 6	—	—	—	—	—	—	—	Retired. Fastest lap 2' 36·7", 190·723 k.p.h. New record.
„	—	Moss	—	—	—	—	2: 3' 45·9"	Front brake locking.
July 13	Moss	—	—	—	—	—	1: 47' 20·38"	Lap record 88·28 m.p.h.
July 19	—	—	—	—	—	—	—	Retired lap 26—broken inlet and exhaust valves.
„	Moss	—	—	—	—	97·92 m.p.h.	44' 50·8"	Fastest lap 1' 46", 99·41 m.p.h.
July 20	Moss	—	—	—	—	93·92 m.p.h.	2: 0' 0·97"	
Aug. 3	—	—	—	—	—	—	—	Retired lap 3—magneto failure. Fastest lap 9' 9·2", 92·9 m.p.h. New record.
Aug. 10	Moss	—	—	—	—	—	1: 25' 21·3"	
Aug. 15	—	Moss	—	—	—	—	58' 29·6"	Lap record 46·7".
Aug. 24	Moss	—	—	—	—	105·03 m.p.h.	2: 11' 27·8"	
Aug. 30	—	Moss	—	—	—	—	41' 0·05"	Fastest lap 57·8", 77·23 m.p.h. 1st in classification.
„	Moss	—	—	—	—	75·84 m.p.h.	41' 12"	Lap record 57·4", 77·77 m.p.h.
Sept. 7	—	—	—	—	—	—	—	Retired lap 18—gear-box seizure.
Sept. 13	Moss	—	—	—	—	88·33 m.p.h.	4: 1' 17"	Record lap 1' 32·6", 93·33 m.p.h. Co-driver Brooks.

1958—*continued*

Date	Club	Circuit	Distance	Event	Formula	Car	H.P.
Oct. 19	R.A.C. Marocain	Casablanca	53 laps 259·1 miles	Moroccan G.P.	I	Vanwall	2496 c.c.
Nov. 29	Confederation of Australian Motor Sport	Albert Park	32 laps 225 miles 100 miles	Melbourne G.P. Heats 1 and 2 Final	I	Cooper	2196 c.c.

1959

Date	Club	Circuit	Distance	Event	Formula	Car	H.P.
Jan. 10	N.Z.I.G.P.	Ardmore	75 laps 150 miles	Auckland G.P.	I	Cooper-Climax	2·2 litre
Mar. 21	Sports Car Club of America	Sebring	12-hours	Sebring 12-hour	Sports	Lister-Jaguar	2986 c.c.
Mar. 30	B.A.R.C.	Goodwood	42 laps 100·8 miles	Glover Trophy	I	Cooper-Climax	2·5 litre
April 8	—	Palais des Sports	—	G.P. d'Europe des Micromils	—	—	—
April 18	B.A.R.C.	Aintree	67 laps 201 miles	Aintree '200'	I	Cooper-B.R.M.	2·5 litre
April 25	A.C. di Siracusa	Madonie	55 laps 188 miles	Syracuse G.P.	II	Cooper-Borgward	1500 c.c.
May 2	B.R.D.C.	Silverstone	—	International Sports Car Race	Sports	Aston DBR1	2992 c.c.
,,	,,	,,	12 laps	Grand Touring Car Race	G.T.	Aston DB4	3670 c.c.
,,	,,	,,	50 laps 2·93-mile circuit	Daily Express Trophy Race	I	B.R.M.	2·5 litre
May 10	A.C. de Monaco	Monte Carlo	100 laps 198 miles	Monaco G.P.	I	Cooper-Climax	2·5 litre
May 31	K.N.A.C.	Zandvoort	75 laps 195 miles	Dutch G.P.	I	Cooper-Climax	2·5 litre
June 7	A.D.A.C.	Nurburg Ring	44 laps 1,000 km.	Nurburg Ring 1,000 km.	Sports	Aston-Martin DBR1	2992 c.c.
June 20/21	A.C. de l'Ouest	Sarthe	24-hours	Le Mans	Sports	Aston-Martin DBR1	2992 c.c.
July 5	A.C. de Champagne	Rheims-Gueux	50 laps 258 miles	G.P. d'Europe	I	B.R.P.-B.R.M.	2·5 litre
,,	,,	,,	25 laps 128·9 miles	Rheims F. II Race	II	Cooper-Borgward	1500 c.c.
July 12	A.C. de Normand	Ròuen Les Essarts	35 laps 143 miles	Rouen G.P.	II	Cooper-Borgward	1500 c.c.
,,	,,	,,	35 laps	Coupe Delamere Debouttville	Sports	Maserati	2000 c.c.
July 18	R.A.C./B.A.R.C.	Aintree	75 laps 225 miles	British G.P.	I	B.R.P.-B.R.M.	2·5 litre
,,	,,	,,	17 laps	Sports Car Race	Sports	Cooper-Climax	2·5 litre
July 26	A.C. d'Auvergne	Clermont-Ferrand	26 laps 130 miles	Circuit of Auvergne	II	Cooper-Borgward	1500 c.c.
Aug. 2	A.C.V.D.	Avus	2 heats of 30 laps each	German G.P.	I	Cooper-Climax	2·5 litre
Aug. 9	Karlskoga M.C.	Karlskoga	30 laps	Kanonloppet	Sports	Cooper-Monaco	2·5 litre
Aug. 15/16	A.S.K.	Roskilde Ring	140 km.	Roskilde Sports Car G.P.	Sports	Cooper-Monaco	2·5 litre
Aug. 23	A.C. de Portugal	Monsanto-Lisbon	62 laps 210 miles	Portuguese G.P.	I	Cooper-Climax	2·5 litre
Aug. 29	B.R.S.C.C.	Brands Hatch	42 laps	Kentish 100—Heat 1 Heat 2 Classification	II	Cooper-Borgward	1500 c.c.

1958

Date	Result				Other Places	Speed	Time	Comments
	1st	2nd	3rd	4th				
ct. 19	Moss	—	—	—	—	116·20 m.p.h.	2: 9' 15·1"	Fastest lap 2' 22·5", 117·8 m.p.h.
ov. 29	Moss	—	—	—	—	98·86 m.p.h.	1: 45'	Fastest lap 102·26 m.p.h.

1959

Date	Result				Other Places	Speed	Time	Comments
	1st	2nd	3rd	4th				
n. 10	Moss	—	—	—	—	82·80 m.p.h.	1: 48' 24·4"	Fastest lap 1' 24·8", 85 m.p.h. (record).
ar. 21	—	—	—	—	—	—	—	Disqualified—ran out of petrol.
ar. 30	Moss	—	—	—	—	90·31 m.p.h.	1: 6' 58"	Fastest lap 1' 31·8", 94·12 m.p.h.
pril 8	Moss	—	—	—	—	—	—	
pril 18	—	—	—	—	—	—	—	Retired—nut worked loose. Fastest lap 1' 58·8", 90·01 m.p.h. (record).
pril 25	Moss	—	—	—	—	99·718 m.p.h.	1: 53' 0·6"	
ay 2	—	Moss	—	—	—	98·23 m.p.h.	44' 41·8"	Class record 1' 45", 100·35 m.p.h. Old record beaten by 4·6 seconds.
"	Moss	—	—	—	—	86·94 m.p.h.	24' 14·4"	Fastest lap 1' 58·8", 88·7 m.p.h.
"	—	—	—	—	—	—	—	Retired—brake failure.
ay 10	—	—	—	—	—	—	—	Retired lap 82—transmission.
ay 31	—	—	—	—	—	—	—	Retired lap 63—gear box. Fastest lap 1' 36·7", 96·99 m.p.h. (record).
ne 7	Moss	—	—	—	—	82·52 m.p.h.	7: 33' 18"	Lap record 9' 32", 89·16 m.p.h. Co-driver Jack Fairman.
ne 20/21	—	—	—	—	—	—	—	Retired—valve trouble.
ly 5	—	—	—	—	8th	—	42 laps completed	Excessively hot weather—retired—spun and stalled. Fastest lap 2' 22·8", 130·21 m.p.h. (record).
"	Moss	—	—	—	—	119·24 m.p.h.	1: 4' 54·2"	Lap record 2' 33·1", 195·207 k.p.h.
ly 12	Moss	—	—	—	—	96·89 m.p.h.	1: 28' 5·8"	Lap record 2' 24·9", 100·98 m.p.h.
"	Moss	—	—	—	—	95·00 m.p.h.	1: 29' 40·9"	5·3 mile Rouen Circuit.
ly 18	—	Moss	—	—	—	89·67 m.p.h.	2: 30' 33·8"	Fastest lap 1' 57", 92·31 m.p.h. New lap record with McLaren.
"	—	—	—	—	—	—	—	Retired lap 13. Lap record 87·60 m.p.h.
ly 26	Moss	—	—	—	—	76·70 m.p.h.	1: 41' 46·1"	Lap record 3' 48·8", 78·73 m.p.h.
ug. 2	—	—	—	—	—	—	—	Retired—gear box.
ug. 9	Moss	—	—	—	—	67·63 m.p.h.	50' 2·8"	Lap record 1' 38·1", 110·092 k.p.h.
ug. 15/16	Moss	—	—	—	—	106·50 k.p.h.	1: 18' 58·2"	46·2 seconds. Lap record with Piper.
ug. 23	Moss	—	—	—	—	95·32 m.p.h.	2: 11' 55·1"	Fastest lap 2' 5·07", 97·30 m.p.h.
ug. 29	—	—	Moss	—	—	—	40' 43·4"	
	—	—	—	Moss	—	—	40' 58·0"	
	—	—	Moss	—	—	—	1: 21' 1·4"	

1959—*continued*

Date	Club	Circuit	Distance	Event	Formula	Car	H.P.
Sept. 5	R.A.C./B.A.R.C.	Goodwood	224 laps	Tourist Trophy	Sports	Aston-Martin DBR1	2992
Sept. 13	A.C. di Milano	Monza	72 laps 257 miles	Italian G.P.	I	Cooper-Climax	2·5 litr
Sept. 26	Cheshire Car Club	Oulton Park	55 laps 150 miles	Gold Cup Race	I	Cooper-Climax	2·5 litr
Oct. 10/11	Times Mirror Corp.	Riverside	200 miles	U.S.G.P. for Sports Cars	Sports	Aston-Martin DBR2	4·2 litr
Oct. 18	Watkins Glen G.P. Corp.	Watkins Glen	100 laps 230 miles	Watkins Glen G.P.	Libre	Cooper-Climax	2·5 litr
Nov. 27	Bahamas A.C.	Nassau	12 laps 54 miles	Governor's Trophy	Sports	Aston-Martin DBR2	4·2 litr
Dec. 2	„	„	—	Nassau Trophy	G.T.	Aston-Martin DB4GT	3·7 litr
Dec. 12	Sports Car Club of America	Sebring	42 laps 218 miles	United States G.P.	I	Cooper-Climax	2·5 litr

1960

Date	Club	Circuit	Distance	Event	Formula	Car	H.P.
Jan. 1	S.A.G.P. Organizers	East London	60 laps 150 miles	South African G.P.	II	Cooper-Borgward	1487 c.
Jan. 9	N.Z.I.G.P.	Ardmore	30 miles	Qualifying heat of N.Z.G.P.	I	Cooper-Climax	2496 c.
„	„	„	75 laps	N.Z.G.P.	I	Cooper-Climax	2496 c.
Feb. 7	Automovil Club Argentina	Buenos Aires Autodrome	80 laps	Argentine G.P.	I	Cooper-Climax	2496 c.
Feb. 28	Automovil y Aero Club de Cuba	Havana	50 laps	Cuban Sports G.P.	Sports	Maserati	2·8 litr
Mar. 19	A.C. di Siracusa	Syracuse	56 laps	Syracuse G.P.	II	Porsche	—
Mar. 26	A.R.C. of Florida	Sebring	57 laps	4-hour Sebring	G.T.	Sprite	998 c.
„	„	„	12-hours	12-hour Race	Sports	Maserati	2·8 litr
April 10	R.A.C. de Belgique	Brussels	35 laps	Brussels G.P. Heat 1 Heat 2 Gen. classification	II	Porsche	1482 c.
April 18	B.A.R.C.	Goodwood	42 laps	Glover Trophy	I	Cooper-Climax	2496 c.
„	„	„	15 laps 36 miles	Lavant Cup	II	Porsche	1482 c.
„	„	„	10 laps 25 miles	Fordwater Trophy	G.T.	Aston-Martin DB4	3·7 litr
April 30	B.A.R.C.	Aintree	50 laps 150 miles	Aintree '200'	II	Porsche	1482 c.
May 14	B.R.D.C.	Silverstone	12 laps 36 miles	G.T. Race	G.T.	Jaguar	3·8 litr
„	„	„	50 laps	Daily Express Trophy	I	Cooper-Climax	2496 c.
May 22	A.D.A.C.	Nurburg Ring	44 laps	1,000 km.	Sports	Maserati	2·8 litr
May 29	A.C. de Monaco	Monte Carlo	100 laps	Monaco G.P.	I	Lotus-Climax	2496 c.
June 6	K.N.A.C.	Zandvoort	75 laps	Dutch G.P.	I	Lotus-Climax	2496 c.
June 18	R.A.C. de Belgique	Francorchamps Spa	—	Belgian G.P.	—	Lotus-Climax	—
Aug. 7	Karlskoga M.C.	Karlskoga	25 laps	Karlskoga G.P.	Sports	Lotus Monte-Carlo	2·5 litr

1959

Date	Result				Other Places	Speed	Time	Comments
	1st	2nd	3rd	4th				
ept. 5	Moss	—	—	—	—	89·41 m.p.h.	6: 00′ 46·8″	Changed car because of fire.
ept. 13	Moss	—	—	—	—	124·40 m.p.h.	2: 4′ 5·4″	
ept. 26	Moss	—	—	—	—	96·29 m.p.h.	1: 34′ 37·2″	Lap record 1′ 41·8″, 97·64 m.p.h.
ct. 10/11	—	—	—	—	—	—	—	Retired—overheating and oil pressure.
ct. 18	Moss	—	—	—	—	82·10 m.p.h.	2: 47′ 44·0″	Fastest lap 1′ 24″, 97·1 m.p.h.
ov. 27	Moss	—	—	—	—	90·18 m.p.h.	35′ 57·0″	
ec. 2	—	—	—	—	—	—	—	Retired. Lap record 82·78 m.p.h.
ec. 12	—	—	—	—	—	—	—	Retired lap 6—gear box.

1960

Date	Result				Other Places	Speed	Time	Comments
	1st	2nd	3rd	4th				
n. 1	—	Moss	—	—	—	—	1: 43′ 56·0″	Fastest lap 1′ 38·75″, 88·51 m.p.h. Fuel injection pipe split on lap 58.
n. 9	Moss	—	—	—	—	—	20′ 45·9″	
„	—	—	—	—	—	—	—	Retired—clutch trouble. Lap record 1′ 21·2″.
eb. 7	—	—	Moss	—	—	—	2: 18′ 26·4″	Took over Trintignant's car, gaining no points for the World Championship.
eb. 28	Moss	—	—	—	—	127·885 k.p.h.	1: 57′ 31·5″	Lap record 2′ 16″, 132 k.p.h.
ar. 19	—	—	—	—	—	—	—	Retired on lap 27 when in lead—E/F. Lap record 1′ 58·8″, 166·666 k.p.h.
ar. 26	—	Moss	—	—	—	—	—	2nd in class—completed 56 laps.
„	—	—	—	—	—	—	—	Gear box trouble.
pril 10	Moss	—	—	—	—	130·186 k.p.h.	1: 13′ 25·6″	Lap record 2′ 4″, 82·11 m.p.h.
	—	—	Moss	—	—	—	1: 23′ 51·6″	Fastest lap 2′ 7·1″, 74·23 m.p.h.
	—	Moss	—	—	—	—	—	
pril 18	—	Moss	—	—	—	—	1: 0′ 17·6″	New circuit record 1′ 24·65″, 102·13 m.p.h.
„	—	Moss	—	—	—	—	22′ 30·6″	
„	Moss	—	—	—	—	83·03 m.p.h.	17′ 20·6″	Fastest lap 1′ 42·8″, 84·05 m.p.h.
pril 30	Moss	—	—	—	—	88·41 m.p.h.	1: 41′ 47·6″	
ay 14	—	Moss	—	—	—	—	—	
„	—	—	—	—	—	—	—	Retired—wish-bone broke while in lead on lap 34.
ay 22	Moss	—	—	—	—	82·83 m.p.h.	7: 31′ 40·5″	Lap record 9′ 37″, 88·48 m.p.h. Co-driver Dan Gurney.
ay 29	Moss	—	—	—	—	67·48 m.p.h.	2: 53′ 45·5″	
ne 6	—	—	—	Moss	—	—	2: 2′ 44·9″	Lap record 1′ 34·4″, 99·36 m.p.h. Wheel burst but continued.
ne 18	—	—	—	—	—	—	—	Crashed whilst practising for Belgian G.P., breaking both legs, nose and crushing 9th vertebra when wheel came off the Lotus-Climax.
ug. 7	Moss	—	—	—	—	67·95 m.p.h.	41′ 8·8″	Lap record 1′ 33·3″, 69·4 m.p.h. Brand new untried car.

1960—*continued*

Date	Club	Circuit	Distance	Event	Formula	Car	H.P.
Aug. 14	A.C. di Portugal	Oporto	55 laps	Portuguese G.P.	I	Lotus-Climax	2496 c.
Aug. 20	B.A.R.C.	Goodwood	108 laps	Tourist Trophy	G.T.	Ferrari	3 litre
Aug. 27	B.R.S.C.C.	Brands Hatch	40 laps	Kentish 100	II	Porsche	1482 c.
,,	,,	,,	10 laps	Redex Trophy	G.T.	Ferrari	3 litre
Sept. 10/11	A.S.K.	Roskilde Ring	—	Danish G.P.	II	Porsche	1482 c.
Sept. 18	St.M.S.C.	Zeltweg	59 laps	Austrian G.P.	II	Porsche	1482 c.
Sept. 24	Cheshire Car Club Ltd.	Oulton Park	60 laps	Gold Cup	I	Lotus-Climax	—
Oct. 2	A.C. di Modena	Modena	100 laps	Modena G.P.	II	Lotus-Climax	1496 c.
Oct. 9	Watkins Glen G.P. Inc.	Watkins Glen	100 laps 230 miles	Watkins Glen G.P.	I	Lotus-Climax	2496 c.
Oct. 15/16	Sports C.C. of California	Riverside	200 miles	Riverside Sports Car G.P.	Sports	Lotus-Monte Carlo	2496 c.
Oct. 23	,,	Laguna Seca	200 miles (2 heats,100 miles each)	Pacific G.P. Heat 1 Heat 2	Sports	Lotus-Monte Carlo	2496 c.
Nov. 20	—	Riverside	75 laps	United States G.P.	I	Lotus-Climax	2496 c.
Nov. 27	Bahamas A.C.	Nassau	—	Nassau Tourist Trophy	G.T.	Ferrari	3 litre
,,	,,	,,	—	Nassau International Trophy	—	Lotus	—
,,	,,	,,	—	Governor's Trophy	Sports	Lotus 19	—
,,	,,	,,	—	Go-Kart Race	—	Go-Kart	—
Dec. 17	—	Killarney	75 laps	Cape G.P.	II	Porsche	1482 c
Dec. 27	R.A.C./G.P. Organizers	East London	80 laps	South African G.P.	II	Porsche	1482 c

1961

Date	Club	Circuit	Distance	Event	Formula	Car	H.P.
Jan. 7	—	Ardmore	15 laps	N.Z.G.P.—Heat 1	Int.C.	Lotus	2½ litre
,,		,,	75 laps	N.Z. Grand Prix.	Int.C.	Lotus	2½ litre
Jan. 21	—	Wigram Circuit Christchurch	47 laps	Lady Wigram Trophy	Int.C.	Lotus	2½ litre
Jan. 29	Australian A.R. Co. Ltd.	Warwick Farm	45 laps	Warwick Farm International	Int.C.	Lotus	2½ litre
Mar. 24	U.S.C.C.	Sebring	59 laps	4-hour Race	—	Austin-Healey Sprite	994 c.
Mar. 25	,,	Sebring	—	12-hour Race	Sports	Maserati 61 (Birdcage)	2·8 litre
April 3	B.A.R.C.	Goodwood	21 laps	Lavant Cup	Int.C.	Cooper-Climax	—
,,	,,	,,	42 laps	Glover Trophy	I	Lotus	1500 c
,,	,,	,,	15 laps	Sussex Trophy	Sports	Lotus-Monte Carlo	—
,,	,,	,,	10 laps	Fordwater Trophy	G.T.	Aston-Martin Zagato	3670 c.
April 9	R.A.C. de Belgique	Heysel	22 laps	Brussels G.P. Heat 1 Heat 2 Heat 3 Classification	I	Lotus	1496 c.
April 16	O.A.S.C.	Aspern	55 laps	Vienna G.P.	I	Lotus	1496 c.
April 22	B.A.R.C.	Aintree	17 laps	Sports Car Race	Sports	Lotus 19	2496 c
,,	,,	,,	50 laps	Aintree '200'	I	Cooper	1496 c.
April 25	A.C. di Siracusa	Syracuse	56 laps	Syracuse G.P.	I	Lotus	1496 c.

1960

Date	1st	2nd	3rd	4th	Other Places	Speed	Time	Comments
ug. 14	—	—	—	—	—	—	—	Disqualified for pushing car wrong way of track—lap 51.
ug. 20	Moss	—	—	—	—	85·58 m.p.h.	3: 1′ 43·2″	
ug. 27	—	—	—	—	11th	—	—	Carburettor trouble.
„	Moss	—	—	—	—	80·35 m.p.h.	19′ 47·4″	
pt. 10/11	—	—	—	Moss	—	—	54′ 50·4″	Gear-box selector trouble.
pt. 18	Moss	—	—	—	—	87·00 m.p.h.	1: 20′ 13·2″	Fastest lap 1′ 16″, 93·9 m.p.h.
pt. 24	Moss	—	—	—	—	93·85 m.p.h.	1: 45′ 54·0″	
ct. 2	—	—	—	—	—	—	—	Retired—valve tappet broke.
ct. 9	Moss	—	—	—	—	105·80 m.p.h. (record)	2: 10′ 2·2″	Fastest lap 109 m.p.h.
ct. 15/16	—	—	—	—	—	—	—	Retired—transmission trouble.
ct. 23	Moss	—	—	—	—	86·40 m.p.h.	—	
	Moss	—	—	—	—	87·30 m.p.h.	—	Lap record 1′ 17·2″.
ov. 20	Moss	—	—	—	—	99·00 m.p.h.	2: 28′ 52·2″	
ov. 27	Moss	—	—	—	—	83·559 m.p.h.	1: 20′ 16·85″	Fastest lap 84·348 m.p.h.
„	—	—	—	—	—	—	—	Retired—bonnet assembly broke.
„	—	—	—	—	13th	—	—	Retired on lap 12.
c. 17	Moss	—	—	—	—	76·00 m.p.h.	1: 57′ 40·8″	
c. 27	Moss	—	—	—	—	89·24 m.p.h.	2: 11′ 2·0″	

1961

Date	1st	2nd	3rd	4th	Other Places	Speed	Time	Comments
n. 7	Moss	—	—	—	—	—	20′ 16·3″	
„	—	—	—	—	—	—	—	Retired on 30th lap. Half shaft broke at weld.
n. 21	Brabham	Moss	—	—	—	—	1: 18′ 7″	Shunted twice—carbs. were half knocked off. Race shortened by 50 miles—rain.
n. 29	Moss	—	—	—	—	79·26 m.p.h.	1: 16′ 33·9″	Fastest lap 80·68 m.p.h. Tremendous heat.
ar. 24	—	—	—	Moss	—	—	—	58 laps completed.
ar. 25	—	—	—	—	—	—	—	Retired after 3 hours—exhaust system. Co-driver Graham Hill. Battery flat—started after 6 mins.
ril 3	Moss	—	—	—	—	90·47 m.p.h.	33′ 25·6″	
„	—	—	—	Moss	—	—	1: 4′ 19·4″	
„	Moss	—	—	—	—	81·57 m.p.h.	26′ 29·0″	
„	—	—	Moss	—	—	—	17′ 26·6″	
ril 9								
	—	—	—	—	14th	—	—	7 laps behind.
	—	—	—	—	8th	—	—	1 lap behind.
	—	Moss	—	—	—	129·822 k.p.h.	46′ 17·0″	Fastest lap 131·412 k.p.h.
	—	—	—	—	7th	—	—	
ril 16	Moss	—	—	—	—	82·021 m.p.h.	1: 10′ 1·6″	New lap record 1′ 12·2″.
ril 22	Moss	—	—	—	—	87·19 m.p.h.	35′ 5·6″	New lap record 90 m.p.h.
„	—	—	—	—	—	—	—	Retired on 3rd lap—bearings went.
ril 25	—	—	—	—	8th	—	—	Magneto trouble. Retired 2 laps from end of race—4 laps behind.

1961—*continued*

Date	Club	Circuit	Distance	Event	Formula	Car	H.P.
April 30	A.C. di Palermo	Madonie	45 miles 10 laps	Targa Florio	Sports	Porsche	2 litr
May 6	B.R.D.C.	Silverstone	80 laps	International Trophy Race	Int.C.	Cooper	2½ litr
„	„	„	25 laps	Sports Car Race	Sports	Lotus-Monte Carlo	—
May 14	A.C. de Monaco	Monaco	100 laps	Monaco G.P.	I	Lotus	1496 c
May 22	K.N.A.C.	Zandvoort	75 laps	Dutch G.P.	I	Lotus	1496 c
May 28	A.D.A.C.	Nurburg Ring	44 laps	1,000 km.	Sports	Porsche	1·7 lit
June 3	B.R.S.C.C.	Brands Hatch	76 laps	Silver City Trophy	I	Lotus	1496 c
June 10/11	A.C. de l'Ouest	Sarthe	—	24-hour Le Mans	Sports and G.T.	G.T. Ferrari	—
June 18	R.A.C. de Belgique	Francor-champs Spa	36 laps	Belgian G.P.	I	Lotus	1496 c
June 24	Canadian R.D.A.	Mosport Park	40 laps	Players 200 Race Heat 1 Heat 2	Sports	Lotus 19	2½ litr
July 2	A.C. de Champagne	Rheims	52 laps	French G.P.	I	Lotus	1496 c
July 8	B.R.D.C.	Silverstone	52 laps	Empire Trophy	Int.C.	Cooper	2496 c
„	„	„	25 laps	G.T. Race	G.T.	Ferrari	3 litr
July 15	B.A.R.C./Daily Mirror	Aintree	75 laps	British G.P.	I	Lotus	1496
July 23	A.D.A.C.	Solitude	25 laps	Solitude G.P.	I	Lotus	1496 c
Aug. 6	A.C.V.D.	Nurburg Ring	15 laps	European G.P.	I	Lotus	1496 c
Aug. 7	B.R.S.C.C.	Brands Hatch	20 laps	Peco Trophy	G.T.	Ferrari	3 litr
„	„	„	76 laps	Guards Trophy	Int.C.	Cooper	2496 c
Aug. 19	R.A.C./B.A.R.C.	Goodwood	109 laps	Tourist Trophy	—	Ferrari	3 litr
Aug. 20	Karlskoga M.C.	Karlskoga	30 laps	Kanonloppet	I	Lotus	1496 c
Aug. 26/27	A.S.K. of Copenhagen	Roskilde	20 laps 30 laps 30 laps	Danish G.P. Heat 1 Heat 2 Heat 3 and Final	I	Lotus	1496 c
Sept. 3	A.C. di Modena	Modena	100 laps	Modena G.P.	I	Lotus	1496 c
Sept. 10	A.C. di Milano	Monza	43 laps	Italian G.P.	I	Lotus	1496 c
Sept. 23	Cheshire C.C.	Oulton Park	60 laps	Gold Cup	I	Ferguson	—
Sept. 30	Canadian R.D.A.	Mosport Park	100 laps	Canadian G.P. for Pepsi-Cola Trophy	Sports	Lotus 19	2496 c
Oct. 8	United States C.C.	Watkins Glen	100 laps	United States G.P.	I	Lotus	1496 c
Oct. 13/15	United States A.C.	Riverside	200 miles	Sports Car G.P.	Sports	Lotus 19	2496 c
„	„	„	—	3-hour Production Car Race	—	Sunbeam Alpine	—
Oct. 22	S.C.R.A.	Laguna Seca	100 miles	Pacific G.P. Heat 1 Heat 2	Sports	Lotus 19	2496 c
Dec. 3/10	Bahamas A.C.	Oakes Circuit	—	Nassau Tourist Trophy	G.T.	Ferrari	
„	„	„	56 laps	Nassau Trophy	Sports	Lotus 19	2496 c
„	„	„	—	Governor's Trophy	—	Lotus	
Dec. 17	S.A.A.C.	Westmead, Durban	89 laps	Natal G.P.	—	Lotus	1496 c
Dec. 26	„	East London	80 laps	South African G.P.	—	Lotus	1496 c

Date	Result				Other Places	Speed	Time	Comments
	1st	2nd	3rd	4th				
April 30	—	—	—	—	—	—	—	Retired on last lap—broken differential. Co-driver Graham Hill.
May 6	Moss	—	—	—	—	87·09 m.p.h.	2: 41' 19·2"	Fastest lap 93·75 m.p.h.
"	Moss	—	—	—	—	102·36 m.p.h.	—	Fastest lap 106·22 m.p.h.
May 14	Moss	—	—	—	—	70·70 m.p.h.	2: 45' 50·1"	Fastest lap with Ginther, 73·05 m.p.h.
May 22	—	—	—	Moss	—	—	2: 2' 14·3"	
May 28	—	—	—	—	8th	—	8: 2' 7·5"	Class win. Retired in 1·7 Porsche. Co-driver G. Hill. Finished race in a 2-litre Porsche—43 laps.
June 3	Moss	—	—	—	—	91·78 m.p.h.	2: 11' 40·6"	New lap record 93·52 m.p.h.
June 10/11	—	—	—	—	—	—	—	Retired—fan blade flew off cutting water pipe.
June 18	—	—	—	—	8th	—	2: 6' 59·4"	
June 24								
	Moss⎫ Moss⎭	—	—	—	—	84·70 m.p.h.	2: 15·8'	Fastest lap 86·40 m.p.h.
July 2	—	—	—	—	—	—	—	Shunted by Phil Hill after a pit stop for brake pipe. Retired on lap 31.
July 8	Moss	—	—	—	—	104·58 m.p.h.	1: 27' 19·2"	Fastest lap 109·31 m.p.h.
"	Moss	—	—	—	—	94·58 m.p.h.	46' 25·4"	Fastest lap 95·95 m.p.h.
July 15	—	—	—	—	—	—	—	Took over Ferguson until black flagged. Retired on lap 44—fractured brake pipe.
July 23	—	—	—	—	—	—	—	Retired on lap 22—gear box.
Aug. 6	Moss	—	—	—	—	92·34 m.p.h.	2: 18' 12·4"	
Aug. 7	Moss	—	—	—	—	82·47 m.p.h.	38' 33·6"	Lap record 83·53 m.p.h.
"	—	—	—	—	—	—	—	Retired on lap 24—gear trouble.
Aug. 19	Moss	—	—	—	—	86·62 m.p.h.	3: 1' 12·0"	
Aug. 20	Moss	—	—	—	—	—	46' 16·8"	Fastest lap with Surtees—1' 30·4".
Aug. 26/27	Moss⎫ Moss⎬ Moss⎭	—	—	—	—	—	59' 28·5"	Fastest lap 42' 8".
Sept. 3	Moss	—	—	—	—	88·08 m.p.h.	1: 40' 8·1"	Fastest lap 59·2".
Sept. 10	—	—	—	—	—	—	—	Retired on lap 37. Started with Ireland's car—wheel bearing broke.
Sept. 23	Moss	—	—	—	—	88·83 m.p.h.	1: 51' 53·8"	New 1½-litre lap record 93·42 m.p.h.
Sept. 30	—	—	Moss	—	—	—	2: 47' 29·0"	Completed 99 laps. Fastest lap 91·72 m.p.h.
Oct. 8	—	—	—	—	—	—	—	Retired on lap 58.
Oct. 13/15	—	—	—	—	16th	—	—	Leading until brake seal trouble.
"	Moss 1st class	—	Moss 3rd overall	—	—	—	—	With Jack Brabham.
Oct. 22	Moss	—	—	—	—	90·30 m.p.h.	—	
"	Moss	—	—	—	—	91·90 m.p.h.	—	
Dec.3/10	Moss	—	—	—	—	80·115 m.p.h.	—	
"	—	—	—	—	—	—	—	Retired on lap 27—rear wishbone.
"	—	—	—	—	—	—	—	Retired.
Dec. 17	—	Moss	—	—	—	—	2: 13' 30·0"	Fastest lap 93·37 m.p.h.
Dec. 26	—	Moss	—	—	—	—	2: 7' 4·9"	